The first Rolling Stones, at the Marquee Club in London, 1963.

THE ROLLING STONES

TEXT BY
ROBERT
PALMER

DESIGN BY
MARY
SHANAHAN

Sphere Books Limited
30-32 Gray's Inn Road,
London WC1X 8JL

First published in Great Britain by Sphere Books Ltd 1984

Copyright © 1983 by Rolling Stone Press

First published in the United States of America by Rolling Stone Press, Doubleday & Company, Inc 1983

TRADE
MARK

Printed and bound in Spain by Printer
industria gráfica s.a.   Barcelona   D.L.B. 2249-1984

Acknowledgments

The editors wish to acknowledge the following people whose help and cooperation were essential to the creation of this book.

Robert Palmer would like to thank Debra Rae Cohen, for her loving encouragement, her insights, and her invaluable editorial advice and contributions; also Jann Wenner, Sarah Lazin, and Patty Romanowski of Rolling Stone Press, for their ideas and their hard work on every stage of this project; Eric Nisenson, for moral support; Pat Rainer, for her Stones talk and Stones tapes; and in the Stones camp, Jane Rose, Paul Wasserman, Art Collins, Earl McGrath, and the Rolling Stones themselves—especially Keith Richards, for his music and his friendship.

Mary Shanahan would especially like to thank Ilene Cherna, Beth Filler, and Christophe Gruner.

The editors of Rolling Stone Press would like to thank Janis Bultman, Holly George, Bill German, Brion Gysin, Kurt Loder, Brant Mewborn, and Susan Murcko. We would also like to express our appreciation to our editor at the Dial Press, Jim Fitzgerald.

Introduction

ROBERT JOHNSON, the black Delta blues singer who died in 1938 after drinking poisoned whiskey, was an evil genius, Lucifer's right-hand man. At least that's what the God-fearing, churchgoing folk of rural Mississippi thought. Even young Muddy Waters, growing up in the Delta in the Thirties, believed the stories after he heard Johnson wailing "Hellhound on My Trail" on a phonograph record. One afternoon when Muddy was in his teens, he spotted the legendary Robert Johnson singing and playing guitar on a small-town street corner. But Muddy was afraid to get a close look, "because," he explained years later, "people said the Devil taught Robert Johnson to play the blues. They said he was a dangerous man."

The blues acquired its sinister reputation because the people who played and listened to it were outcasts, even within the black community. They were people who shunned preachers as hypocrites and called churchgoers fools, preferring to put their faith in the conjure men and root doctors who were keeping the old African religions alive. And since they'd been branded evil by the proper folk around them, the blues people began to wonder: What *is* evil, anyway? Is it nothing more than the reverse image, the flip side, of good? And if good means the hypocritical values of the proper folk, their tremulous faith and Protestant work ethic and all the rest of the bourgeois baggage handed down by the slave masters—if *that's* all good is, the blues people reasoned, then evil just might be worth investigating.

Several decades later, the Rolling Stones would come to similar conclusions. To Brian Jones, Keith Richards and Mick Jagger in particular, evil as society defined it would begin to seem rich, mysterious and ever so alluring, and rock & roll would be the perfect medium for investigating it.

"The blues had a baby," sings Muddy Waters, "and they called it rock & roll."

Rock & roll had come bursting onto the English scene in the late Fifties, when the Stones were growing up, and Keith, Mick and Brian had been smitten, along with future Stones Bill Wyman and Charlie Watts. But by the early Sixties, Keith has recalled, "the initial wham had gone out of rock & roll." The strongest, strangest music was to be found on those rare records from the Chess label in America —blues records.

It was at England's first blues club, the Ealing Club, in London, that Mick and Keith met Brian. The three young musicians moved into a ratty little low-rent apartment on the outskirts of the Chelsea district and began playing and talking, listening to records and practicing, night and day. They learned to play their own brand of blues, and they learned so well that they were able to coax hard-working pros Charlie and Bill to join them. Brian named their new band the Rolling Stones, after a Muddy Waters song, "Rollin' Stone," a revision of the traditional "Catfish Blues."

Like most of their fellow English blues fanatics, the nascent Stones were beatniks, dropouts, ex-students who chose to devote their lives to the sounds on those treasured, blue-labeled discs from Chicago. What exactly did they hear? What hit them first was raw emotion, men singing until they were hoarse and squeezing moans from guitar strings till their fingers bled. Blues is more than a style, it's a language that expresses the whole range of emotions, from sadness to blind hatred to sheer, crazed lust. The slurs and rasps in the singing, the bending of the notes, the deliberate fluctuations in rhythm and tempo—all these blues techniques are designed to unlock and unleash emotions. The heavier the rasp, the more pronounced the bend, the deeper the feeling— a legacy of the music's roots in Africa, where spoken language is rich in tone, and the lower one pitches a phrase, the more feeling it conveys. All this the Stones themselves discovered in the process of picking those records apart.

But there's another dimension to the blues, the wilder, more mysterious and alluring dimension that links it with voodoo and things that go bump in the night—rhythm. Bo

Diddley, who made records for Chess along with Elmore James and Muddy Waters, hit on something deeply compelling that came to be called the "Bo Diddley beat," a chunky distillation of voodoo and blues rhythms. It was the same thing an African or Cuban or Haitian drummer connects with when he's playing the rhythms that put people into trance. The Stones couldn't have said just what that something was, not in the early days. Yet they knew Bo Diddley had it, and they learned his rhythms thoroughly. The young Stones even played Muddy Waters and Buddy Holly songs with a dark Bo Diddley undertow. They had felt the power of the rhythm, and when they unleashed it at their early gigs, they heard their audiences scream and moan. They realized what they had, and they played it for all it was worth.

The Stones' backbeat has long been the most resilient in rock. It makes some people shiver, but others (like the more than two million paying fans on the band's 1981 American tour alone) hear it and dance for joy. In Africa and in the African-derived cultures of the Americas, the same rhythms that Christians fear as voodoo, the Devil's work, are used by priests and shamans to heal wounds and cure sickness, to bring light and balance to diseased minds and peace and prosperity to entire communities. Brian heard similar rhythms in the village of Jajouka, Morocco, and wanted to integrate them into the Stones' sound, but it wasn't really necessary. The Stones already had the beat.

The Stones appeared on England's pop music scene in 1963, just when the Beatles (and other Merseybeat groups) were reviving the careening energy of Fifties rock 'n' roll, and ever since, the two bands have been inextricably linked. Like the Stones, the Beatles loved black American music, too, but it wasn't the same black music. Their love was for black pop—Little Richard, early Motown—reasonably well-known music that appealed to both white and black Americans. The Stones were different. The music they cared about was as unfamiliar to most Americans—white and black—as it was to all but a handful of Britishers. And their belief in the purity and depth and power of that music gave the Rolling Stones a sense of mission that was to carry them through the next two decades, through the best of times and through some of the very worst of times, too.

As white boys determined to make the blackest of black musical styles their own, the Stones fell prey to contradictions that have torn less determined souls apart. But from the first, they were more than simply blues fanatics, much more. For one thing, they were wildly ambitious; they wanted everyone to feel the power in their music. By the end of their second decade together, it seemed that almost everyone had.

In England in the early Sixties, the Rolling Stones learned to play the blues mainly by listening to the recordings of Muddy Waters and other black bluesmen, all of them Robert Johnson's spiritual sons. By the end of the decade, the Stones had released an album called *Their Satanic Majesties Request*, written and recorded a song called "Sympathy for the Devil" and witnessed a fan's murder at a speedway known as Altamont, by a gang who called themselves the Hell's Angels. Plenty of people in those days thought the Stones were evil geniuses, Lucifer's right-hand rock & roll band. Some people think so still. "There are black magicians who think we are acting as unknown agents of Lucifer," Keith Richards said in a 1971 interview, "and others who think we are Lucifer. Everybody's Lucifer."

Like the bluesmen who were their models, the Rolling Stones became town criers, articulating whatever their audience was thinking and feeling but hadn't been able to put into words. Their songs were always honest, and they often sang openly about sex and drugs when other popular performers were still carefully disguising such references with code words and innuendo. They asked hard questions and refused to settle for easy answers. In fact, they never pretended to have answers. Like the bluesmen, they gave their audience hard-hitting reportage fresh from the current social and sexual and political battlefields, poetry and healing rhythms—and voodoo incantations aimed at bringing the society of pious platitudes, napalm and newspeak crashing down around their feet. They were hell-bent Robert Johnsons, hard-boiled Raymond Chandlers, sexually explicit Henry Millers, scatological Louis-Ferdinand Celines and hallucinating-on-the-road Jack Kerouacs, all rolled up into one explosive—and possibly dangerous—rock & roll band.

MICK JAGGER

(born July 26, 1943), the son of a physical-education instructor, grew up middle class in Dartford, one of London's more distant suburbs. Keith Richards (December 18, 1943) spent his early years living near his friend Mick, but his father went from job to job. Keith was eleven when the family decided to economize by moving into subsidized housing and a rougher neighborhood on the other side of town. When the future Glimmer Twins were in their early teens, Mick was building his body and thinking about a respectable career, while in the housing project, Keith was learning to fight in order to protect himself from the neighborhood bullies and Teddy boys. And then rock & roll struck: first Bill Haley's "Rock around the Clock," which was wildly exciting, then Elvis Presley, who was something more. Sexy, self-confident, a man's man, a woman's man and a guitar-toting musician, Elvis represented a new and intriguing combination.

Although the two had long lost touch, both Mick and Keith practiced their Elvis moves in front of their mirrors. They also latched onto some rock & rollers who weren't as well known in England—especially Chuck Berry and Bo Diddley, both black guitarists and singers who recorded for Chess. During the late Fifties and early Sixties, when most of the English kids who'd been wowed by Presley were gamely trying to get excited about clean-cut teen idols Cliff Richard and Billy Fury, Mick and Keith were following another trail, like two detectives working independently from the same clues. Berry and Diddley led them back to Muddy Waters and Little Walter, whose records were hard to find in England. Mick, always a self-

starter, solved that problem by writing directly to Chess Records, Chicago, U.S.A. He was carrying some of the records the company had sent him when he ran into Keith on the train one day in 1960. Their mutual interest in the music helped rekindle their friendship.

Brian Jones (February 28, 1942) grew up in Cheltenham, a quiet, tidy resort town. His family, more solidly middle class than either Keith's or Mick's, encouraged him to get a good education and select a lucrative, dignified profession, perhaps medicine or law. But Brian began listening to the Dixieland or trad jazz that was England's most popular alternative to rock & roll in the late Fifties, and taught himself to play various instruments, most notably saxophone and guitar. He discovered a network of coffee shops and jazz clubs extending throughout his corner of western England, and when he played there, serious, intense young girls who dressed in black and read poetry looked at him with adoration and longing in their eyes.

During the early Sixties, some of the more ambitious trad-jazz musicians discovered that their music's roots were in the blues, and once Brian heard Elmore James and Muddy Waters, he was hooked. By 1962, when he read that a blues club had opened in London, he was playing James' style of slide guitar, fretting the instrument with a metal slide or bottleneck to produce that speechlike Delta whine. He hitchhiked to London, where he listened to an older, ex-trad guitarist named Alexis Korner and his band, Blues Incorporated, play at the Ealing Club. They were hot, but Brian knew he was already in their league and he asked if he could sit in. Before long, he was a regular there, and one night when he stopped in to play, Mick and Keith were in the audience and introduced themselves. They were still amateurs, and Brian had considerable professional experience. But the three clicked, and soon after, when Brian left

Brian Jones was the Stones' perennial outsider. Bill Wyman, Charlie Watts, Mick Jagger and Keith Richards (on following pages) all grew up in the suburbs around London, but Brian was from Cheltenham—"a very genteel town full of old ladies," Keith later recalled, "where it used to be fashionable to go and take the baths once a year at Cheltenham Spa…It's a Regency thing, you know, Beau Brummel, around that time. Now it's a seedy sort of place full of aspirations to be an aristocratic town. It rubs off on anyone who comes from there." Dartford schoolmates Jagger and Richards renewed their childhood friendship one day in 1960 —"of all places, on the fucking train," said Keith. Jagger was going up to the London School of Economics. He had some American R&B records with him and Keith was very impressed. "He was born my brother by accident by different parents," said Mick. "We're very close."

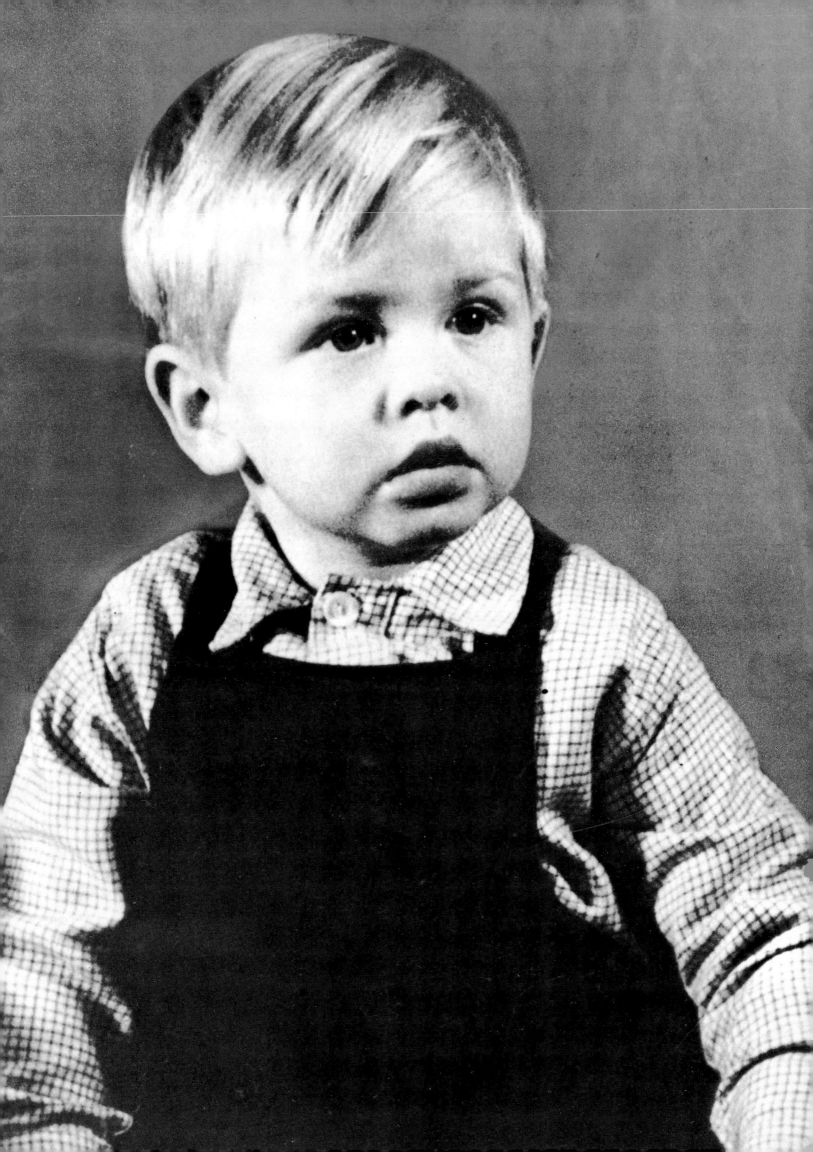

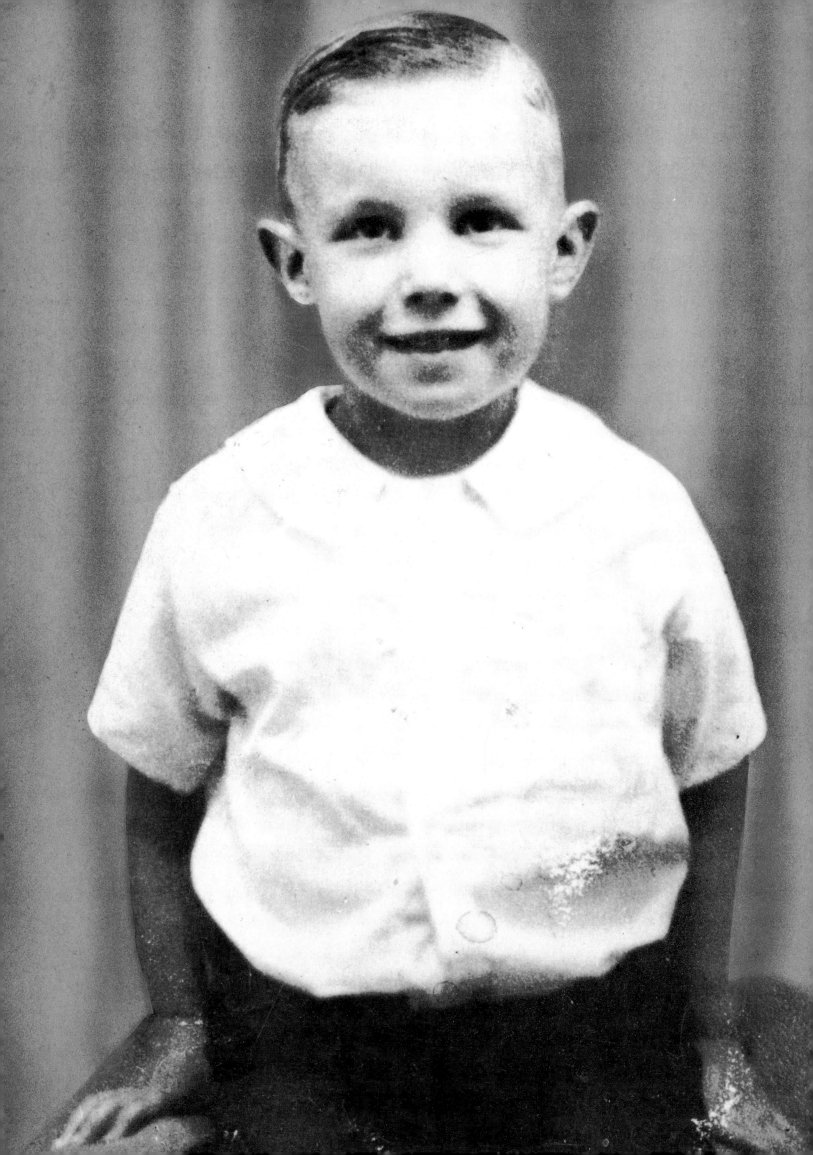

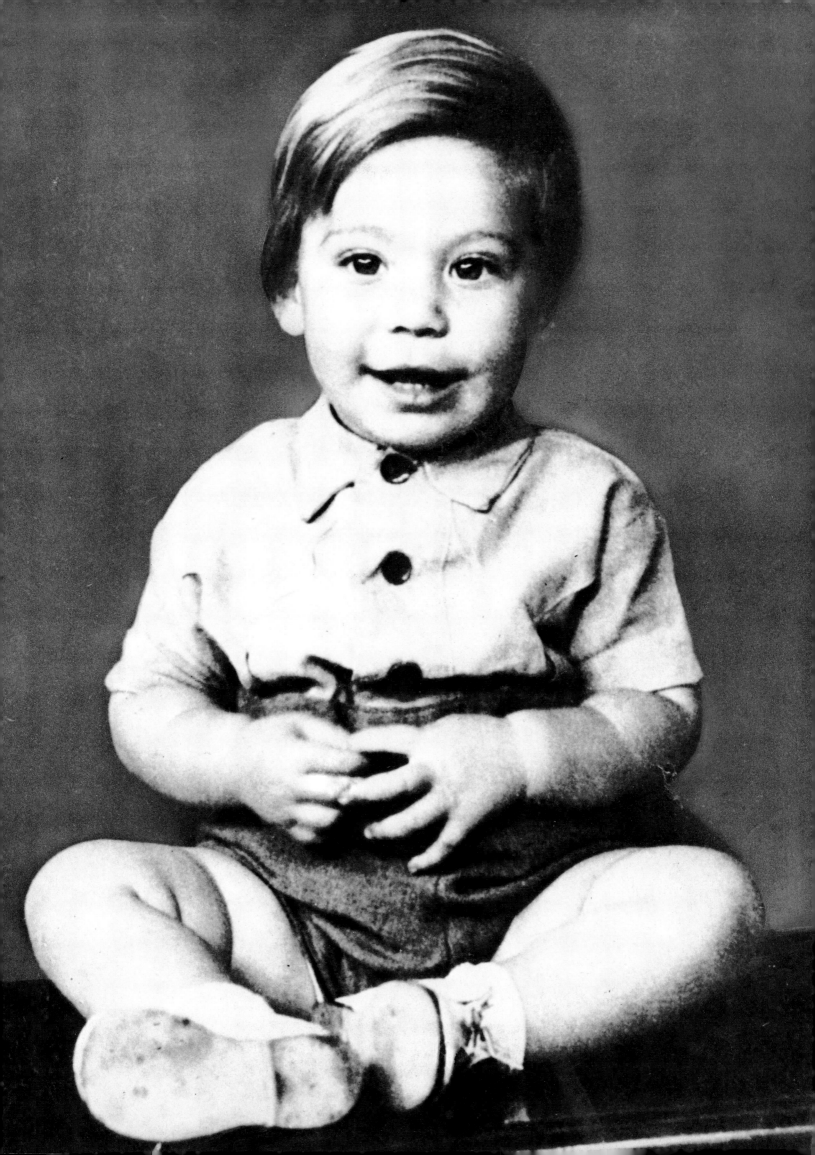

Previous pages: Mick fronting
Alexis Korner, Jack Bruce, Cyril
Davies and—unseen, but surely
not unheard—Charlie Watts in
Blues Incorporated at the Ealing
Club, circa 1962; and Mick
with Brian and Keith, cutting
up with fan photos of the kind of
teen idols they themselves would
soon become. Right: Onstage in
1963, a little stiff and ripe for
the arrival of young PR hustler
Andrew Loog Oldham, who became their manager.

Just 'cause you feel so good,
   do you have to drive me
   out of my head?
I said, hey you get off of my
   cloud, hey you get off of
   my cloud,
Hey you get off of my cloud,
   don't hang around
'Cause two's a crowd on my
   cloud baby.

[Get Off My Cloud]

Cheltenham for London, he moved into the grungy Chelsea apartment with Mick (by now a student at the London School of Economics) and Keith.

They drank and chased girls together, pooled their record collections and their talents. If necessary, they would spend weeks listening to the same records over and over to figure out how Bo Diddley's rhythms worked, or why Jimmy Reed's apparently simple shuffle beat was so difficult to reproduce. Brian amazed Keith and Mick by learning to play passable blues harmonica in one day, and while Mick was in school, Brian and Keith would work on their guitars until the two of them could lock their parts together and play like one man. By early summer of 1962, Brian, Keith and Mick were rehearsing with another friend, Ian Stewart, a pianist with a natural feel for boogie-woogie, bassist Dick Taylor (later founder of the Pretty Things) and drummer Mick Avory (later with the Kinks).

On July 12, they played their first gig as the Rolling Stones at a second London blues club, the Marquee, which had opened after the Ealing Club proved blues music would draw crowds.

Bill Wyman (October 24, 1936), a bassist who worked with several rock

At the height of homeland Beatlemania, Andrew Oldham orchestrates the anti-Beatles. Only nineteen years old himself when he signed them, Oldham knew what the Stones wanted— and he wanted some too.

The Look: an outtake from the
photo session that produced the
cover for Out of Our Heads. As
the Daily Mirror mused: "Everything seems to be against
them on the surface. They are
called the ugliest group in Britain....But an awful lot of people
love 'em—those five, shaggy-as-
Shetland-ponies lads known as
the Rolling Stones."

23

Preceding pages: Keith demonstrates natural Stones style, and Bill, Mick and Brian demonstrate Oldham's idea of Stones style during their first TV appearance, on England's "Thank Your Lucky Stars," in June 1963. (The slick look was swiftly discarded.) Left: More TV, cooler threads.

& roll groups and held down a day job to support his family, took Dick Taylor's place later that year. And in January 1963, the Stones replaced Mick Avory with Charlie Watts (June 2, 1941), whose buoyantly swinging work with Alexis Korner and Blues Incorporated they had long admired. Watts worked days, too, in an advertising agency. It was a long shot for Watts and Wyman, joining a group of scruffy blues fanatics who were viewed with some suspicion even by other purists. Their hair was too long, they looked as if they needed to bathe more regularly, and their taste in music was not only more obscure than what English blues fans were used to, but more polluted by rock & roll. Still, there was something there—a certain drive, a sense of mission, a penetrating wit and intelligence, and a feel for the music that seemed deeper and less studied than that of folkie types like Alexis Korner.

Mick had been sitting in with Korner and Blues Incorporated since early 1962, and Brian was a popular guest musician at Korner's gigs. The blues players around Korner couldn't understand why two of their most talented acolytes would want to play with Keith, who never disguised his love for Chuck Berry and other rock & roll guitarists. But Mick, Brian and Keith were so sure of themselves that they ignored the advice they were getting from Korner and friends. Once

With Oldham, left, and Gene Pitney and Phil Spector, right, at the "Not Fade Away" session, Regent Sound Studios, London. Right: Nights to remember, 1963.

Well I'm sick and tired
And I really have my
    doubts.
I've tried and tried
But it never really works
    out.
Like a lady in waiting to a
    virgin queen;
Look at that stupid girl.
She bitches about things
    that she's never seen.
Look at that stupid girl.
It doesn't matter if she dyes
    her hair
Or the color of the shoes she
    wears
She's the worst thing in this
    world.
Look at that stupid girl.

[STUPID GIRL]

they'd lured Wyman and Watts into the fold, they knew they were ready to roll.

In February 1963, budding impresario and blues lover Giorgio Gomelsky hired them to play weekly at the Crawdaddy Club in the London suburb of Richmond. There, the Stones were able to build their own audience from scratch. In the beginning, British blues had attracted a thoughtful, polite crowd of art students, budding beatniks and older jazz fans, along with a few more casual listeners who'd come to blues through trad jazz. Rock & roll was for Teddy boys, roughnecks, juvenile delinquents; trad jazz was for sophisticates and, despite its somewhat raunchier sound, so was Blues Incorporated. The Stones still sat on stools to play when they opened at the Crawdaddy, which was actually the back room of a pub in

Ecstasy as an environment, 1964. By April, rioting and fainting at Stones concerts was front-page news in England, and a regular enough occurrence to prompt considerable public debate. Also that month, their first album unseated the Beatles at the top of the charts.

Richmond's Station Hotel. But they didn't remain seated for very long, and neither did the students and artsy dropout types who came to hear them. Soon Mick was up shaking maracas or a tambourine, Brian was shaking his outrageously long blond mop in front-row faces, and the fans were standing on chairs and tables, shaking to the pulsating rhythms. The Stones' sets left audiences sweaty, exhausted, but curiously elated. This was no ordinary band.

Brian and Mick, the band's most outgoing performers, were otherwise very different. Brian played to the girls in the audience, nailing the prettiest ones with eye contact. Mick was still shy, but he had those strange, big, pouty lips, and when he shook his thin hips, some of the girls thought he was sexier than Brian. Keith, who stood off to one side playing his guitar, already had the raffish look of a highwayman. Bill, dark and saturnine, older than the others and a family man, seemed utterly disdainful of everything but the bass lines with which he firmly anchored the music. Charlie drummed away, looking tough and enigmatic.

They were disparate personalities, these five, but already they had a chemistry, a special balance, a group identity. Brian, nominally the band's leader, was a dedicated student of the blues, determined to get the music right, but

Preceding pages: Mania in Manchester, August 10, 1964. A prototype for the arena-rock culture that was to come: band late performing, kids caught in crush at front of the stage, et cetera. "Dozens of girls fainted," said the Daily Mirror, "some even before the group appeared." Right and below: It took over a dozen police to pry them away from fans following an appearance on TV's "Ready, Steady, Go!," and they still lost the door to their Austin Princess in the panic. "One of the most horrifying mobbings we've ever had," said Mick.

If you ever plan to motor
    west,
Travel my way, take the
    highway, that's the best
It winds from Chicago to
    L.A.
More than two thousand
    miles all the way.
Get your kicks on Route 66.
You go through St. Louis,
    Joplin, Missouri,
And Oklahoma City looks
    mighty pretty.
You'll see Amarillo, Gallup,
    New Mexico,
Flagstaff, Arizona, don't
    forget Winona,
Kingman, Barstow, San
    Bernardino.
Won't you get hip to this
    timely tip?
When you make that
    California trip,
Get your kicks on Route 66.

[ROUTE 66]

he was also determined to make the Stones a commercial success. Mick was cool, bright, analytical, with commercial ambitions of his own. That made him a perfect complement to Keith, who did things mostly by feel. Bill was quiet unless he was having a few drinks with his closest friends, but he was as reliable as his playing. He watched Mick and Keith and Brian argue among themselves about which songs to play or which directions to take with a slightly cynical smile; when they finally finished thrashing it out, he'd find a simple but rock-solid bass part that fit and offer a bit of soft-spoken encouragement. Charlie was

mercurial, a little moody, and not one to waste words. When he did open his mouth, though, he always said something incisive and sensible, and the whole band listened. Both he and Bill were content to be the rhythm section, team players. Neither had any desire to argue with Brian, Mick and Keith about what to play or which way to move. Like Bill, Charlie was always supportive, but when the others needed a kick in the rear end—usually when the music or their egos began to drift out of control—Charlie would hit a rim shot or make a withering remark and get them back on track.

When the Stones opened at the Crawdaddy Club, they were a sextet that included burly pianist Ian Stewart. It was a group of purists—and then again, it wasn't. On one hand, the Stones went to any length necessary to seek out the most potent black music from America, listening avidly to musicians almost none of their fans had heard of. "I hope they don't think we're a rock & roll outfit," Mick said earnestly in mid-1962. And two years later, when the Stones were the hottest band in England, Brian Jones was still purist enough to remark, "The essential difference between ourselves and the British groups that are well known in the United States at the moment is that . . . we haven't adapted our music from watered-down music like white American rock & roll. We've adapted our music from the early blues forms."

Yet unlike most other purists, the Stones weren't content just learning about the music of their heroes, or even with learning how to play it idiomatically. They were determined to play the music for as many people as possible, and to make them like it. And they believed in the music, and in themselves, with such conviction that they *knew* they could bring it off. This paradox—the most recondite purism versus the most intense ambition—is at the heart of the Rolling Stones. Earlier white blues musicians never imagined there could be more to playing the

Taking America by bus. The Stones toured the States twice in 1964. Andy Warhol and Tom Wolfe administered their cultural christening at New York's Academy of Music and Ed Sullivan presented them to the nation on his Sunday evening television show. London's bad boys were making good—their first album hit high on the U.S. charts.

blues than playing as much like their black idols as was humanly possible. They understood their own purism as a set of limits, and they stayed well within those limits. But the Rolling Stones knew early on that learning to accurately reproduce phrases and rhythms and entire records was only the *beginning*; they learned everything they could about the blues because they knew they would find freedom in their knowledge—the freedom to play their own blues.

From the first, the paradox of purism versus ambition gave the Stones' music the dynamic tension that enabled them to become just what they set out to be: the band that popularized the deepest blues and went on to make something from it that was entirely their own. Brian felt this tension with particular intensity. The Stones' virtuoso traditionalist, he was able to summon the bite of Muddy Waters' slide guitar, the ringing, bell-like tones of Elmore James or the slurred, moaning harmonica sound of Little Walter with breathtaking verisimilitude. But he was also the Rolling Stone most driven by dreams of pop-star glory, the first to recognize the group's potential to compete successfully with the Beatles.

Mick and Keith learned to make the paradox work for them by writing songs. Together, they were able to create an original musical style by building on blues structures and inflections. Even after the band's sound began to stray from blues basics, the frankness and juice and unsentimental view of life that had so attracted them to the form was never far from the surface. Brian never worked out the paradox that was so central to the Stones ethos. He never learned to write songs of his own—at least, not ones the Stones could perform. He remained conflicted about the need to progress musically and the need to remain faithful to his roots, and the conflict eventually tore him apart.

Even in 1963, during the early days at the Crawdaddy, Brian's inner de-

Brian Jones surveys the sexual wonderland from the stage in San Bernardino, hottest stop on the Stones' first U.S. tour. "Mick went through his camp period in 1964," said Keith. "Brian and I immediately went enormously butch and were sort of laughin' at him."

bate was causing problems. He had named the Rolling Stones and made many of the decisions about musical direction. Giorgio Gomelsky, who soon began to serve the band as a voluble, unofficial manager, dealt with Brian as the leader, and the other Stones seemed to go along. But Gomelsky could never be quite sure. Occasionally, Brian would make an unpopular decision, and when that happened, the others would simply ignore him.

Though Brian, Keith and Mick were still living together and seemed to be the best of friends, there were shifting alliances, snits and paranoia within this unholy trinity. Brian had been severely asthmatic as a child and was still subject to sudden attacks. That made him nervous and jumpy, and he was wildly insecure as well. He compensated for his feelings of inadequacy by asserting his leadership, often in self-centered, childish ways, like asking for a larger share of an evening's pay or for other favored treatment. And there was a desperate edge to his insistent ego. He *needed* to think of himself as undisputed leader of the Rolling Stones—and not without reason. His back was against the wall.

For starters, his Cheltenham girlfriend, Pat Andrews, had followed him to London, bringing their infant son, Julian (named by Brian for the jazz saxophonist Julian "Cannonball" Adderley). Brian was attempting to support Pat and Julian with his meager earnings as a musician, and he was determined to win the approval of his parents, who still expected him to be a success. Add to these pressures a complicated and unsettled love life, with Pat complaining bitterly about his other girlfriends, and it's easy to see why Brian identified so strongly with darkly driven bluesmen like Robert Johnson and Elmore James. He knew he wasn't suited for a job in the nine-to-five world, he felt cornered, and, as his main man Elmore James wailed, there was only "One Way Out." He would become a pop star. That way, he

could support Pat and Julian in style, mollify his parents and spend most of his time touring, recording and shuttling willing young lasses in and out of his hotel rooms.

The other Stones *looked* lean and hungry (except for the stocky pianist Ian Stewart), but Bill and Charlie still had their day jobs to fall back on, and Mick had only recently dropped out of the London School of Economics. Keith wasn't working or studying outside the band, but he was young and footloose, and his mother was still bringing him a stack of freshly laundered shirts once a week. All the Stones wanted to make the band work, only Brian was in a hurry.

On April 21, 1963, the Beatles taped their first television appearance on "Thank Your Lucky Stars," and stopped by the Crawdaddy afterward to hear and meet the Stones. A week later, Andrew Oldham, a bright nineteen-year-old publicist who'd talked his way into a job handling the Beatles' press relations, was in the Crawdaddy audience. Oldham was well connected and on the make. He has insisted that from that first night, he understood the Stones' commercial potential, knew they could become his very own anti-Beatles—and there is little reason to doubt him. Before the following week was out, he had drawn up an exclusive management agreement and talked the Stones into signing it.

Brian saw Oldham as a gift from heaven, the answer to his problems with Pat and Julian, his parents and money. And it was Brian who pushed hardest for the deal, against the advice of Gomelsky, who counseled them to hold out for more control, especially control of their recording career. Still, it didn't take the Stones very long to decide for themselves that Oldham was at least a good bet. He was their own age, full of ideas and drive and blessed with street smarts, too. He was honest enough to admit that his contacts wouldn't be sufficient to make the Stones a pop sensation, and he had

Private lives: right, Mick with girlfriend Chrissie Shrimpton en route to Ed Sullivan. Overleaf: the "super-private world of the Rolling Stones" revealed in 16 *Magazine. Following pages: Brian Jones in Hollywood and Linda Lawrence, the early girl-friend he deserted, at her Berkshire home in September 1965 with their son Julian.*

WELCOME to the super-private world of the Rolling Stones — where never an "outsider" has been allowed to tread! Since the Stones don't consider you 16-ers outsiders (but rather the "in"-est of the "ins"), they are cordially opening the doors to their very own homes and inviting you in for a visit, a look and a chat.

The first Stone place we stop by is Mick Jagger's secret hideaway in the heart of London. He has just moved there and is already getting complaints from his neighbors about the frequent and rather noisy visits he gets from screaming fans!

Mick's living room is quite simple. He has black and white "op" draperies lined with red, oak wood-work and parquet, a white rug and white walls.

"How's for a spot of tea?" Actually, Mick digs into grapefruit while he shows you his over-sized tea cups of Canton design.

Furniture collector Jagger poses by his favorite possession — a huge gilt-framed mirror. On his left is his portable stereo set, and his bed and end tables are reflected in the mirror.

Rolling Stones

C'mon along and drop in on
Mick and Brian
at their London hideaways.

STONE "sitarist" and guitarist (also has been known to sing harmony and even lead!), bouncy Brian Jones lives in an adorable cottage in a mews street in the Chelsea section of London. Brian's "pad" is world-famous among the pop stars as the place where there's always a groovey party going on. Many is the night when such notables as John Lennon, Bob Dylan, the Spoonful and the other Stones are seen coming and going from Brian's friendly little white house.

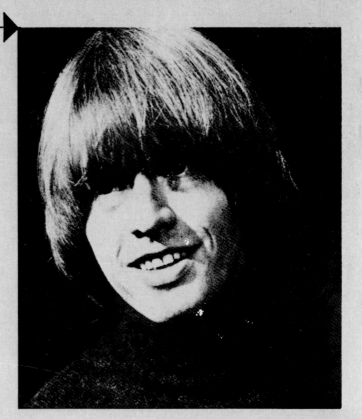

This is what Brian's home looks like from the outside. He says, "I keep planning to plant something in those window boxes — but, then, I'm actually too lazy!"

How's this? A personal serenade just for you from Brian Jones himself! This is where Brian spends most of his spare time — on the floor in front of his hi-fi.

Or — wait a min! — flopped on his bed making phone calls. (Brian's bedroom is done all in white, except for the heavy orange drapes.) Looks like we caught him in the middle of calling up some bird!

Be sure to get the November issue of 16 Magazine — it goes on sale September 20th — and continue 16's exclusive visit to the homes of the Rolling Stones.

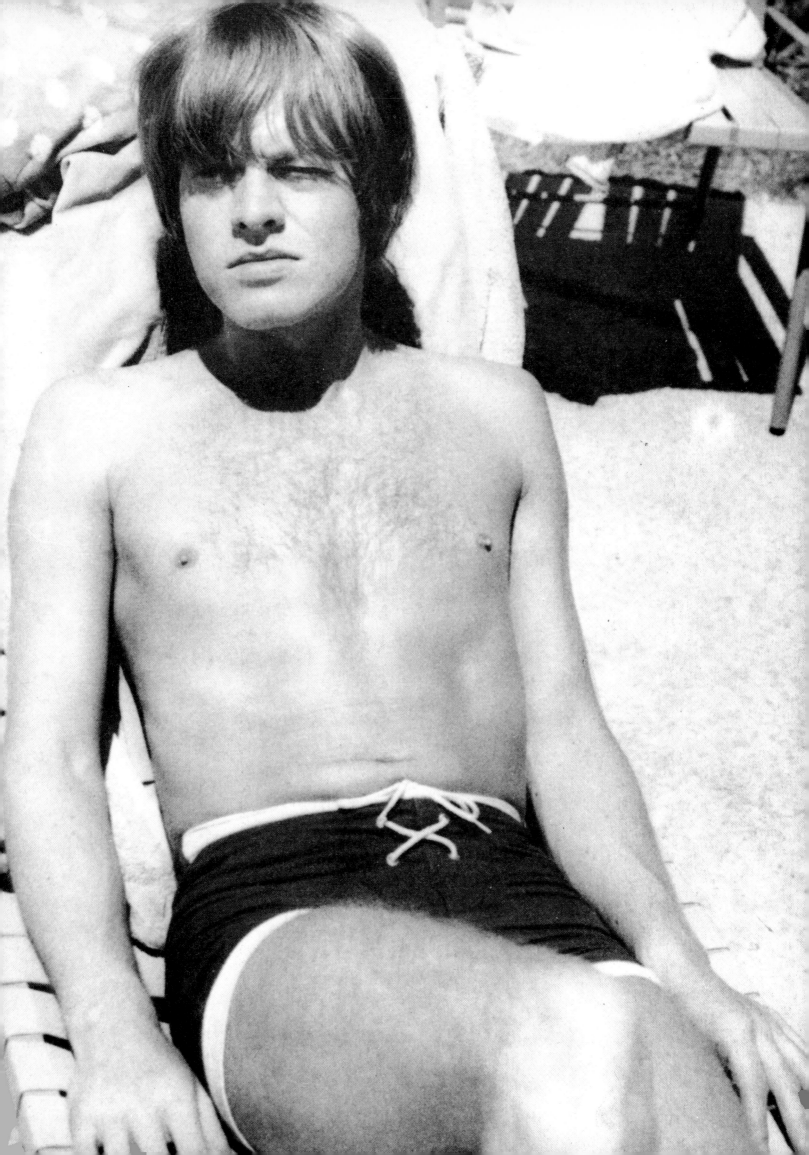

Left, the group at mid-decade. Following pages: Charlie Watts tends his public image prior to a TV appearance, and England's Queen magazine proclaims the new Beatles.

a solution—Eric Easton, a middle-aged mill owner with money to invest and first-name friendships with theater owners throughout the British Isles that dated from his early days as a theater organist. Together, Oldham and Easton convinced the Stones that fame and fortune were practically around the corner, and they signed on the dotted line.

Easton's taste in pop music ran to crooning and other styles predating rock & roll, and while he could appreciate the Stones as instrumentalists and crowd pleasers, he simply couldn't take Mick's singing seriously. At first he wanted to drop Mick from the lineup. The always reasonable Ian Stewart helped talk him out of that—and was rewarded by being dropped himself. As far as Oldham was concerned, Stu neither looked nor acted like a Rolling Stone, and besides, five faces and names were already too many for the teenage fans to remember and identify with. Brian could have argued the point, but he chose to go along, and convinced the others that they should do likewise. Stewart stayed on the payroll as road manager and occasional pianist, keeping his hurt and resentment well hidden. But he never really forgave Brian.

The Stones had already made a few recordings with a young engineer named Glyn Johns, but Oldham bought back the tapes with Easton's money. A week after signing their management contract, the Stones were in London's Olympic Studio, recording their first single, for Decca Records. Their timing couldn't have been better. With the Beatles already the freshest pop sensation in years, Decca was more than willing to shell out a substantial advance for another self-contained, longhaired band—especially one that had already attracted favorable notice in the press and had a devoted club following as well. The fact that the Stones played blues and R&B and were bohemians who always looked flagrantly unkempt did not seem to bother Decca's executives. Long hair and beat groups were too new, too different. The Beatles, a symbol of rebellion to many of their teenage fans, were inspiring riots and hysteria everywhere they went, yet many parents couldn't help finding them cute, in their matching mop-top haircuts and identical suits. Their style and their success were unprecedented. Decca's executives could hardly be blamed for failing to see the subtle distinction between the two groups.

Arriving in New York for yet another U.S. tour, 1965. Right: Charlie ponders the ascension of the Beatles—newly named Members of the Order of the British Empire—into sedate society.

A crowded day for the Beatles

Redundancy Payments

The world's greatest rock & roll
band, earning its title. Overleaf:
Bill and Charlie, older than the
others, the Stones' team players.

When I'm watchin' my T.V.
And that man comes on to
   tell me
How white my shirts can be.
Well, he can't be a man
'Cause he doesn't smoke
The same cigarettes as me.

When I'm ridin' 'round the
   world
And I'm doin' this and I'm
   signin' that
And I'm tryin' to make
   some girl
Who tells me, baby
Better come back later next
   week
'Cause you see I'm on a
   losing streak.
I can't get no, oh, no, no, no
Hey, hey, hey, that's what I
   say.
I can't get no satisfaction,
I can't get no girl action,
And I try and I try and I try
   and I try
I can't get no, I can't get no.

[SATISFACTION]

The powers that be at Decca also failed to note—or perhaps did not care —that Oldham had never produced a record and had no idea what it involved. But Oldham's inexperience actually worked in the Stones' favor. The Beatles had been bashing out cover versions of Fifties rock 'n' roll hits in tough waterfront bars and were happy to let their musically literate producer, George Martin, polish them, shape their sound and their arrangements and gradually transform them into a pop group. The Stones' musical abili-

ties and their ambitions were better matched. They played hard-driving, gutsy music that would brook little polishing. What they needed was a more or less impartial observer who might tighten them up a bit but would concentrate on choosing the most commercial songs from their stage repertoire and making sure they captured some of the excitement on tape. The Stones were a little nonplussed when Oldham, utterly in the dark as to what mixing was all about, blithely left this crucial final step in the recording process to the engineer. But what the hell; for the time being, the sound quality of Stones discs would have to take care of itself.

For their first single, Oldham and the band chose the Chuck Berry song "Come On," an anthem of frustration with an undercurrent of surly rebellion. The song had another advantage as well; Berry's original version had never been released in England. The Stones rushed the song so badly the first time they worked on it that they had to schedule another session, and even the version they finally released didn't really please them. ("It was shit," said Jagger some years later.) But the disc's release in June 1963 coincided with the heady beginnings of rampant Beatlemania and the Merseybeat rock-group boom. Oldham's experience publicizing the Beatles' early releases helped, too. "Come On" climbed to Number Twenty-one on the British charts, and the Stones were on their way.

"Come On" has a loping, two-beat rhythm that's a little reminiscent of Jamaican ska, but it never seems to settle comfortably into a groove. Mick sounds nervous, and the corny key change in the bridge is worthy of a provincial lounge combo. But at least the Stones were trying to be different. They knew, if only intuitively at first, that it would be pointless to try to duplicate their idols' recordings as authentically as possible. They also knew that if they rethought the music, es-

pecially rhythmically, they could come up with interpretations that were as valid as the American originals.

"Come On" wasn't a particularly inspired example of the band's rhythmic revisionism, but by the time the Stones returned to the studio in September, they were confident enough to capture at least some of the flash and momentum of their club sets. Their second stab at the Chuck Berry song book, "Bye Bye Johnny," which was included on the Stones' first four-song EP in January 1964, was a flat-out rocker, with Brian and Keith dovetailing two syncopated, hard-edged rhythm guitar figures into Bill and Charlie's eight-to-the-bar boogie beat and Mick sounding supple, relaxed and absolutely confident. The other songs cut at these early sessions were a mixed bag of blues, soul and black rock & roll tunes. The muddy, distorted "Money" and Mick's adenoidal vocal on the band's first try at Leiber and Stoller's "Poison Ivy" were unintentionally comical, but Arthur Alexander's "You Better Move On," a crowd favorite at live shows, was given a spare, thoughtful pop-soul treatment.

John Lennon and Paul McCartney provided the Stones with their first big hit and inspired them to take up songwriting. Within a few years, Lennon and McCartney would revolutionize pop music by making self-contained groups, original songs and continual experimentation and innovation not just the fashion but the norm. But in 1963, their motivation for creating their own material was still primarily economic. There was plenty of money in songwriting royalties, which explains why Lennon and McCartney were eager to sell the up-and-coming Stones on an original tune they had no immediate use for themselves: "I Wanna Be Your Man." The Beatles eventually recorded it as a vocal feature for Ringo. The Stones turned it into a wildly careening riff tune, and it rocketed into the Top Fifteen, helped along by the opening salvos of Oldham's pub-

licity campaign and by the Stones' first national package tours. Their third single, an inventive recasting of Buddy Holly's "Not Fade Away," made it to Number Three early in 1964 and began to stir up interest in the band in the United States.

Among the earliest American Stones fans were the rock & roll stars who headlined on their initial English tours, and who later opened for the Stones after they became headliners early in 1964. Bo Diddley hung out backstage with Brian and Keith when the Stones opened a Diddley/Everly Brothers package tour and marveled at their confident handling of his signature beat. Brian was particularly adept at getting Diddley's sound and feel on the guitar, without sounding like a mere imitator; he spoke the language fluently and idiomatically. The most impressive evidence of this is "Mona," a highlight of the Stones' first album. The cut is dominated by a deft, mercurial dialogue between Brian's tremolo guitar and Charlie's jungle tomtoms; Mick's grainy vocal seems to float in a sea of reverb and compelling cross rhythms.

The Everly Brothers' keening mountain harmonies and strummed acoustic guitar riffs seem to have left a more lasting impression on Keith. The electric power-chord riffing that is his most distinctive contribution to the art of rock & roll rhythm guitar is rooted in the acoustic guitar figures that powered Everlys hits like "Bye Bye Love," "Wake Up Little Susie," "Bird Dog" and "When Will I Be Loved?"

The Ronettes also became Stones fans when they were second-billed on the band's first headlining tour. Mick and Keith actively competed for lead singer Ronnie Spector's affections, despite a telegram from her husband, American record producer and pop tycoon Phil Spector, advising them, "Stay away from my girls." Spector flew to London in late January, probably to keep an eye on Ronnie and the other two Ronettes. But the Stones and Oldham quickly drew him into their orbit, and he was an enthusiastic participant in the February sessions for the first Stones album. He huddled in a corner with Mick to bang out a song, "Little by Little," that was eventually credited to Spector and the entire band under its collective pseudonym, Nanker Phelge. He shouted encouragement while the Stones recorded a Booker T-like organ instrumental, with Brian wailing a harmonica lead and Keith contributing a stinging guitar solo. "Phelge" called the tune "Now I've Got a Witness (like Uncle Phil and Uncle Gene)" when it appeared on the album. And Spector was a key instigator of the drunken horseplay that led to the recording of "Andrew's Blues," a pornographic ditty that recounted Oldham's sexual exploits, satirized Decca president Sir Edward Lewis and became the first of the Stones' legendary unissued nasties, the original "Cocksucker Blues."

Although Spector's presence must have given the Stones and their tyro producer considerable confidence, he never was much of a musical influence. The Wagnerian melodrama and meticulous layering of his wall-of-sound productions were the antithesis of Oldham's laissez-faire studio philosophy, and of the Stones' tendency simply to try each song several different ways until a particular tempo and arrangement seemed to click. *The Rolling Stones*, which was released by English Decca on April 26, 1964, is pure, unvarnished Stones, from its startling cover, a darkly lit group photo with neither title nor band name on it, to the music, a canny mix of electric blues, black Fifties rock 'n' roll, contemporary soul hits, the prerock boogie-woogie of "Route 66," the Phelge and Phelge-Spector numbers and Mick and Keith's modestly dire "Tell Me," which is partially redeemed by Keith's rangy, over-the-top backing vocals.

This first Stones album is a record of the band's early stage repertoire and a seminal white-rock LP. The Stones

themselves have expressed, with reservations, some fondness for it. "We were kids, you know, just kids," Mick demurred in a 1968 interview in *Rolling Stone* magazine. "We were blues purists who liked ever so commercial things but never did them onstage because we were so horrible and so aware of being blues purists.... You could say that we did blues to turn people on, but why they should be turned on by us is unbelievably stupid. I mean, what's the point in listening to us doing 'I'm a King Bee,' when you can hear Slim Harpo doing it?"

If you're listening to Mick, there isn't much point in rehearing "King Bee" when Harpo's swamp-blues original is available. Mick's vocal is an earnest, not particularly convincing homage; even the spoken asides are copped from the Harpo version. But Keith's flat-picked rhythm figures, Brian's slide-guitar and harmonica leads, Bill's fluid, buzzing bass glissandi and Charlie's understated backbeat owe little to Harpo's loose, rambling swamp-blues sound. And the other blues on the album get equally distinctive instrumental treatments.

Yet while the blues numbers on *The Rolling Stones* are some of the best ever recorded by a white band, the soul numbers are conspicuously inferior. Soul music like "Can I Get a Witness" requires a gospel-trained singer's style and grit, and Mick had neither the power to bring this off nor the technique to fake it. His voice sounds thin, his pitch uncertain, and the rest of the band, so imaginative when putting its fresh stamp on blues material, can't come up with anything better than bland, piano-dominated shuffles.

The A sides of the singles the Stones released between their next single, "Not Fade Away" (February 1964), and their breakthrough "Satisfaction" (May 1965) are a more accurate chart of the band's evolution than the English and American album releases, which had somewhat different contents and running orders right up to

Brian tried to compensate for Mick and Keith's increasingly tight hammerlock on the Stones' music and image by living that image to the hilt. And the group's burgeoning legion of frenzied fans (overleaf) loved it.

Their Satanic Majesties Request in 1967. (Albums released on their American label, London Records, were shorter; some, like *December's Children*, contained tracks from earlier albums and material from English EPs. Before the Stones started recording *Satanic Majesties*, Oldham and the group dissolved their business relationship. From then on, Stones albums were the same on both sides of the Atlantic.)

"Not Fade Away" proved the Stones could make acoustic music as hard-edged and pungent as their most heavily amplified numbers, but "It's All Over Now" (June 1964), a song originally recorded by young Bobby Womack and his group the Valentinos, was something else, a quantum leap forward. On "It's All Over Now," the Stones' awesome twin-guitar firepower is plainly felt, and Keith unleashes the first of the great power-chord riffs with which he was about to revolutionize rock rhythms. It's the two-beat chordal figure he plays just after Mick sings "I used to love her," and although it sounds like pure Keith Richards today, it's just the sort of dramatic, stripped-down lick that served as the rhythmic linchpin on uptempo Everly Brothers singles.

Keith's caterwauling backup singing on "It's All Over Now" is a far cry from the Everlys' refined harmonies, but it does have a white country-music flavor, and so does the modified Merle Travis-style picking Keith layers on top of Brian's strutting rhythm guitar part just after Mick finishes each chorus line with the words "but it's all over now." The rhythm section is strong but subtle, and the vocals are mixed a bit lower in relation to the instrumental track than on previous singles. The entire performance has a tightness, a unity that makes "It's All Over Now" the first incontestably great Stones single. It's no accident that it was also the first Stones single recorded in America, at Chess studios in Chicago during the group's first American tour in 1964.

Mick and Keith and Andrew recording "Satisfaction" at RCA Studios in Hollywood, during the Stones' 1965 tour. "It was Keith, really," said Mick. "I mean, it was his initial idea. It sounded like a folk song when we first started working on it, and Keith didn't like it much. He didn't want it to be a single, he didn't think it would do very well. That's the only time we have had a disagreement."

Phil Spector helped the Stones book studio time at Chess, where Muddy Waters, Bo Diddley, Chuck Berry and other Stones favorites had recorded. Waters and Berry dropped in to listen and offer encouragement; they were glad these weird English upstarts were recording their songs, both for the songwriting royalties that would come their way and for the exposure Stones covers would give their music. At Chess, the band recorded its next English singles, "It's All Over Now" backed with "Good Times, Bad Times," then "Little Red Rooster." The latter track features Brian's slide playing and a Jagger vocal that's full of nuance, dripping with sex and unsettled by an undercurrent of menace. "Rooster" remains one of the Stones' favorites from among their early recordings. Despite the fact that it was a Number One hit in England, "Little Red Rooster" was never released in America as a single; it later appeared on *The Rolling Stones, Now.* In any event, "Rooster" was the group's last blues single. The followup, "The Last Time" (February 1965), was a chugging rocker, a little slower than "It's All Over Now" but with a similarly tight mesh of interlocking guitar parts and a taste of the earlier single's country flavor, especially in Keith's high harmony singing. "It's All Over Now" had been the Stones' first Number One single in England. "The Last Time," their third British Number One (after "Little Red Rooster"), was also their first hit single written by Jagger and Richards. Their subsequent singles were all Jagger-Richards originals; the next one, released six months after "The Last Time," was "Satisfaction."

IT'S easier to trace the musical evolution of the Stones' sound through their singles than it is to detail the changes success wrought in their lives. They have never given a blow-by-blow account of their activities during 1964 and the first half of 1965, probably because those eighteen months passed in a frantic blur. They were working almost constantly. They began 1964 with their first tour as headliners. By April, rioting and fainting at Stones concerts were front-page news in England, and a regular enough occurrence to prompt considerable public debate. In May, their first album toppled *With the Beatles* from the top of the English charts after selling 100,000 copies on the day of its release. On June 1, they began their first American tour, despite the fact that their biggest American hit, "Not Fade Away," had only climbed into the Eighties on the charts. They played to houses that were almost empty, and in private, they were suffering a major failure of nerve. But they carried on, working hard to excite the fans who did show up and making network television appearances, enduring the gibes of hosts like Dean Martin. And once they had recorded in Chicago and Los Angeles, they knew they could make powerful records with the kind of gutsy sound they had admired on releases by black artists but hadn't been able to achieve to their satisfaction in English studios. They did not record in England again until the 1966 sessions for *Between the Buttons.*

After zipping off to Paris, where their French fans rioted, the Stones returned to the U.S. in October for a second American tour. Ed Sullivan booked them onto his show for the first time, pop artist Andy Warhol and writer Tom Wolfe came to see them at New York's Academy of Music, and by the end of October, they were headlining the star-studded TAMI (Teen Age Music International) Show in Santa Monica, California, following James Brown, Chuck Berry and what seemed like half the Motown stable. Their first album had finally penetrated the American Top Fifteen. London Rec-

ords had titled it *England's Newest Hitmakers* and slapped a banner with those words and the group's name on it over the original titleless, wordless cover.

January 1965 found the Stones touring Ireland and Australia, and at the end of the month, Decca released their second English album, *Rolling Stones No. 2*, most of which was recorded in Chicago. In America, London squeezed two more albums (*12 x 5* and *The Rolling Stones Now*) out of the material on the first two English albums and two English EPs, but some tracks didn't appear in America until years later, most notably the Muddy Waters blues "I Can't Be Satisfied," one of Brian's slide-guitar masterpieces. The track eventually saw the light of day in the U.S. on the 1972 compilation *More Hot Rocks*.

Most of the songs on *No. 2* were still covers of black American records, and again, the quality was uneven. There were fine blues and some magnificently moody soul ballads; "Time Is on My Side" first appeared on *Rolling Stones No. 2*. There were also a few near-disasters, particularly the awkward "Under the Boardwalk." Mick and Keith weren't yet setting the world on fire as songwriters, but at least their contributions to *No. 2* ("What a Shame," "Grown Up Wrong" and "Off the Hook") were suitable vehicles for the tough, metallic ensemble sound they were now getting with the help of engineers Ron Malo of Chess and Dave Hassinger of RCA Studios in Hollywood.

In March 1965, England's Number One album, EP and single were all by the Rolling Stones, and the Stones and Beatles were warily eyeing each other's release schedules before deciding the best time to put out their next discs. In April, the Stones started their third American tour, and during the ensuing weeks, Keith came up with and then refined the riff that became the basis of "Satisfaction." They

The titular hero of Charlie Is My Darling, *an abortive film the Stones attempted to make while playing Ireland in September 1965. Said Oldham, "Looking back, it seems like it was just an exercise in bullshitting ourselves. We just wanted to be able to see the credits. Then we said, 'We'll go on with this,' but we never did."*

worked on the song throughout the tour and finally recorded a version that suited them in early May, at RCA in Hollywood. According to Mick, "it sounded like a folk song when we first started," a protest song influenced by Bob Dylan. But by the time the Stones were through, Keith's fuzz-tone guitar riff, the charging Memphis rhythm and Mick's teasing, deliberately difficult-to-make-out vocal were its distinguishing features. In the U.S., the single jumped from Number Sixty-four to Number Four in just two weeks, and shortly after that, it became the Stones' first American Number One. It repeated this success when it was released in England at the end of August, and it subsequently topped charts around the world.

"I can't get no satisfaction" was a cry of frustration and impatience that anyone could understand. Making out some of the other lyrics was more difficult, but dedicated listeners, their ears glued to tinny car radio speakers or to the tweeters on their home stereos, thought they heard Mick sing about "trying to make some girl," only to have her tell him "baby, better come back early next week, 'cause you see, I'm on a losing streak. . . ." Millions of adolescents decided this was a thinly disguised menstrual reference and blushed or snickered; like the epochal "Louie Louie" a few years earlier, "Satisfaction" provided a generation of fresh-faced teenagers entree into an arcane but absolutely fascinating new world of grown-up sexuality. For many listeners, that's what "Satisfaction" was all about—discovering sexual mysteries to the accompaniment of a tough fuzz-tone guitar riff and a compelling beat.

But anyone who'd been listening to the Stones for a year or two knew they usually had more on their minds than a beat and a smirk. "He can't be a man 'cause he doesn't smoke the same cigarettes as me" wasn't a veiled reference to smoking grass, as many thought. It was a warning that, with basic values like manhood bound up in something as ephemeral as the marketing of new products, satisfaction is going to be in short supply. "Satisfaction" works as a classic rock single, but it also asserts that tensions and frustrations are *inherent* in a capitalist society with consumerist values. In other words, "Satisfaction" is a Trojan horse—a quasi-Marxist critique of consumerism and its cost to society and to the individual, disguised as a mindlessly sexy rock & roll song.

Redlands was the name of the fifteenth-century, thatched-roof manse Keith bought in Sussex in 1966. "Whose boat is that?" asked a visiting journalist. "Oh, that belonged to the owner, I bought it off him," Keith replied. "You can paddle round the moat in it..."

T HE success of "Satisfaction" neatly brings down the curtain on the first phase of the Stones' career. Although they had taken off on their first headlining tour of England only eighteen months earlier, a lot had changed, both musically and in terms of the balance of power within the band. Perhaps the most important change had been the emergence of Mick and Keith as the Stones' songwriters and *de facto* musical directors, and with it Brian's inevitable fall from grace. Onstage, Brian had always competed with Mick for the fans' attention. He would stop playing his guitar in the middle of a song, begin bashing a tambourine and suddenly lunge toward the lip of the stage, an evil smile illuminating his impish countenance and the alarmingly dark circles under his eyes, his mane of blond hair tossing violently from side to side. Mick was a fluid, sexy dancer, and with Brian vying for the spotlight as well as leadership of the band, he drove himself relentlessly.

"Mick went through his camp period in 1964," Keith later recalled. "Brian and I immediately went enormously butch and were sort of laughin' at him." But not everyone noticed the difference. There was considerable speculation as to whether and how many of the Stones were perverts, and Oldham cannily encouraged the ambiguity. With his prominent red lips and almost girlish figure, Mick was attracting male as well as female groupies. He also appealed to straight young men who didn't want to admit he was sexy but got a tingle from his act nevertheless. A few blues singers had exploited a certain sexual ambiguity, and it's common among voodoo doctors and shaman types in general. But it was something new in American show

You know I'm smiling, baby,
You need some guiding, baby,
I'm just deciding, baby,
Now I need you more than ever
Let's spend the night together,
Let's spend the night together now.

This doesn't happen to me ev'ry day,

No excuses offered anyway.

I'll satisfy your ev'ry need.
And now I know you will satisfy me
Let's spend the night together
Now I need you more than ever
Let's spend the night together now.

[LET'S SPEND THE NIGHT TOGETHER]

business, and if it sold records, the Stones were willing to go along with it. The whole trip reached its zenith in 1966 when the entire band posed in matronly drag for the cover of the single "Have You Seen Your Mother, Baby."

In packaging the Stones, Oldham did more than simply emphasize unisex. He'd set out to make them the group parents would love to hate, the group that was evil and threatening rather than cute, like the Beatles. A newspaper headline asking "Would you let your daughter go out with a Rolling Stone?" was a typical Oldham brainstorm, and whenever there was

June 1966: The Stones depart London for another U.S. tour. In Syracuse, New York, they scuffled with police who objected to their dragging an American flag across the floor of the War Memorial Hall. The Stones said they only wanted it for a souvenir, and allegedly apologized.

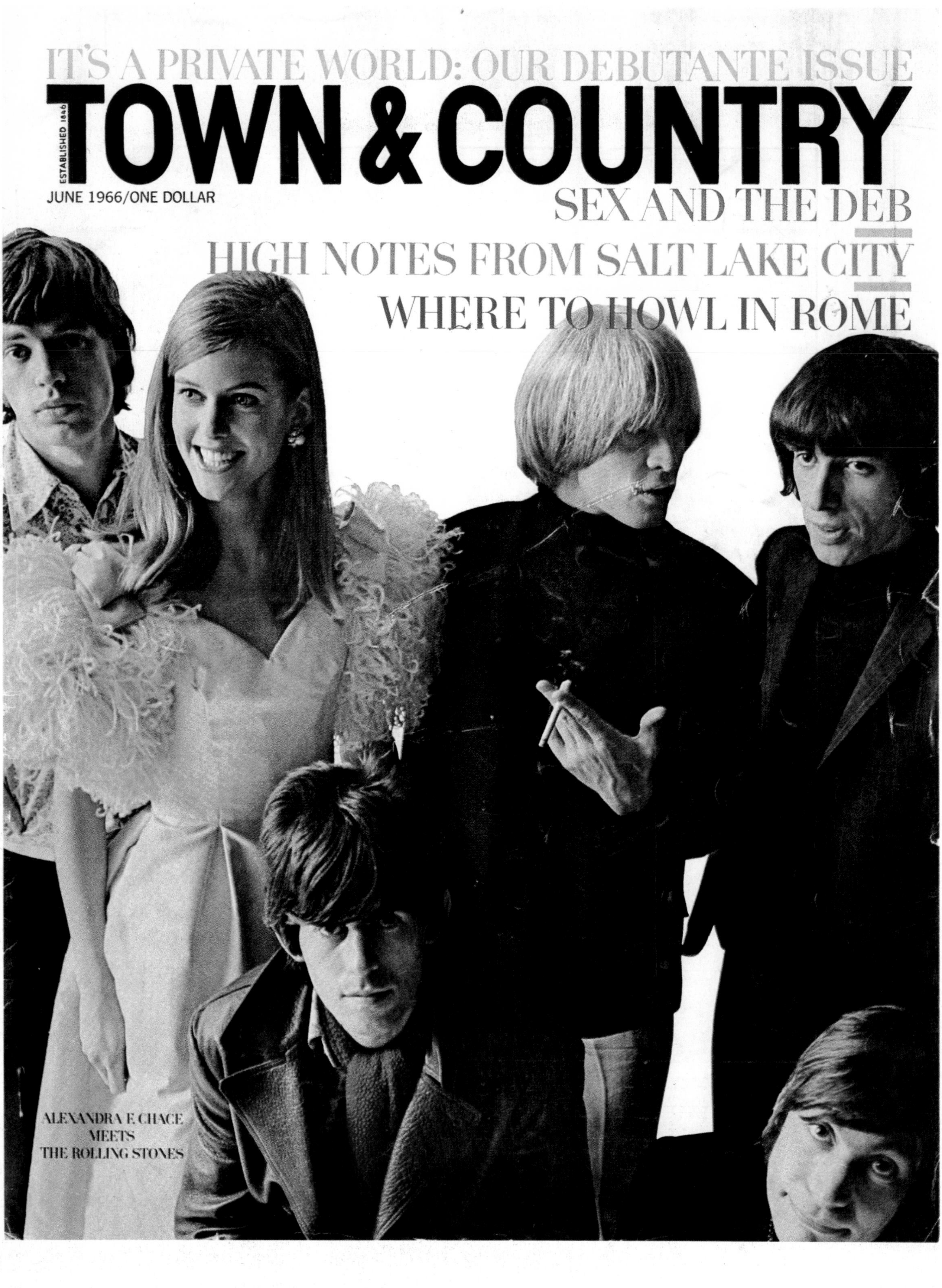

IT'S A PRIVATE WORLD: OUR DEBUTANTE ISSUE

TOWN & COUNTRY

ESTABLISHED 1846

JUNE 1966/ONE DOLLAR

SEX AND THE DEB

HIGH NOTES FROM SALT LAKE CITY

WHERE TO HOWL IN ROME

ALEXANDRA E. CHACE
MEETS
THE ROLLING STONES

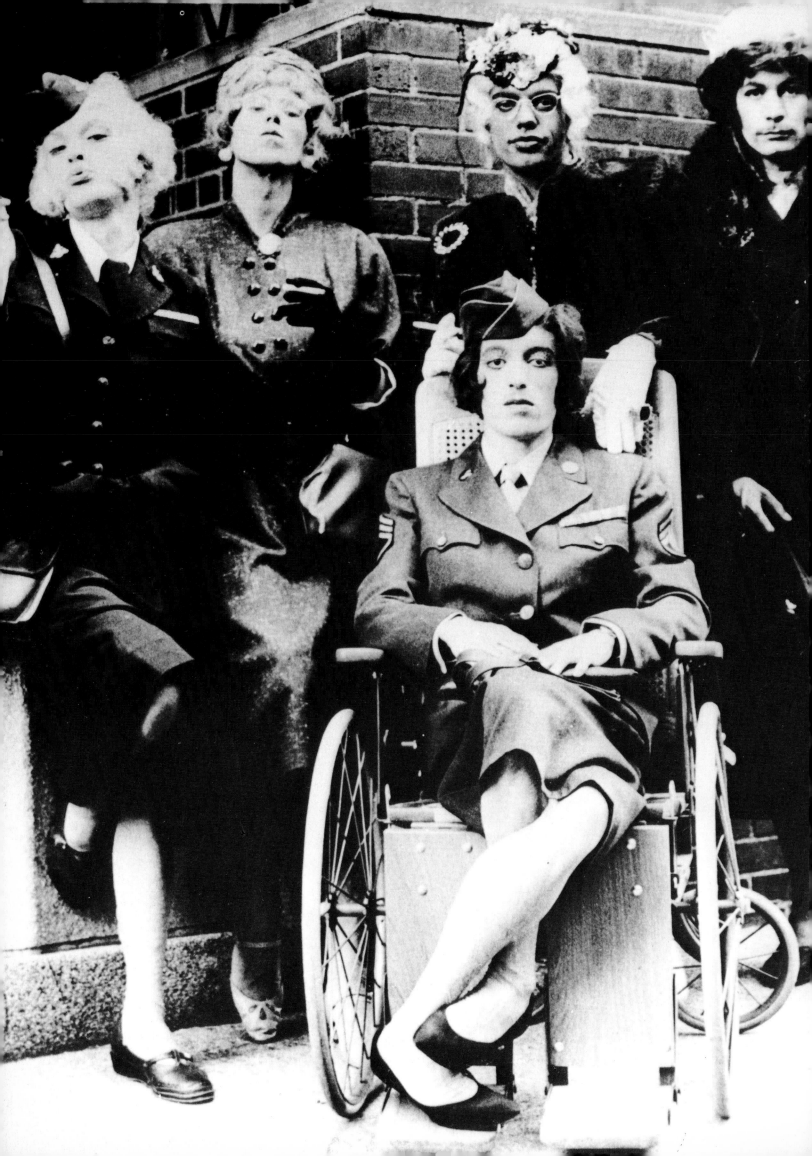

Tell me a story about how
  you adore me,
How we live in the shadow,
  how we see through the
  shadow,
How we glimpse through
  the shadow, how we tear
  at the shadow,
How we hate in the
  shadow and love in your
  shadowy life.

Have you seen your lover,
  baby, standing in the
  shadow?
Have you had another baby
  standing in the shadow?
Where have you been all
  your life?
Talking about all the people
  who would try anything
  twice.

[HAVE YOU SEEN YOUR MOTHER,
  BABY]

an incident he thought he could exploit —like the evening several group members were arrested for urinating against a service-station wall—he played it up for all it was worth. Brian, who'd always been fastidious about his grooming, was chagrined when the press called his band a bunch of filthy Neanderthals. But as long as Oldham was making them famous and showing signs of making them rich, Brian was the last to object.

In the studio, Brian was at least as important as any other Stone to the success of the early singles. The months he had spent with Keith in the Chelsea flat, working out a bluesy ensemble style that bypassed the conventions of rhythm and lead playing and harked back to some of the earliest country blues guitar duets, enabled the band to get a taut, tightly meshed sound in which each player's part was equally in the forefront. When there was room for a solo, Keith handled the rock & roll breaks, usually with a variation on a Chuck Berry routine, but Brian's slide guitar and harmonica dominated on the bluesier material. And Brian also fulfilled another ensemble function, one that emphasized harmonics or overtones.

On "The Last Time," for example, his guitar provided a chugging rhythmic figure and also filled out the sound with ringing but slightly muffled harmonics, sounding like an almost subliminal keyboard. His harmonica often echoed like a reedy organ and seemed to haunt the spaces between the other instruments' parts. Later on, Brian achieved similar effects with dulcimer, Mellotron and various flutes and reed instruments. His instrumental conception was intuitively orchestral and helped give the Stones' sound a presence and depth that many other guitar bands lacked.

The varied musical tasks Brian set himself, and the sexual attention he commanded so effortlessly, would have been enough for many musicians, but not for him. He was making money, sending plenty back from the road to support his son, Julian, while bedding down with as many female admirers as he could handle. His face was prominent in the most striking band photos, and he often spoke for the group to interviewers. But Brian wanted more, and though he might not have been able to say exactly what else he required, he did know that the more the Stones came to depend on the Jagger-Richards songwriting partnership for hits and musical direction, the more his claims to be leader of the band became a hollow joke. He complained to various girlfriends that Mick and Keith were conspiring to throw him out of the Stones, and the more paranoid and withdrawn he became, the more the others avoided or made fun of him, thus fanning the flames. He seemed genuinely incapable of writing finished songs of his own. He did manage to get some sweet, naively mystical poetry down on paper, and he actually may have set some of it to music. But although he told a number of people he was writing songs, and even provided titles for a few of them, he seems never to have played any of them for the other Stones, or for more than a few friends outside the group.

Apparently, Brian did sing a few of his songs for Linda Lawrence, who became his live-in girlfriend after his final breakup with Pat Andrews. She remembered them as being "songs . . . like Donovan's—about his feelings." If the poetry quoted in *Death of a Rolling Stone: The Brian Jones Story* is typical of what Brian was writing, his reluctance to show it to the other Stones is understandable. "The scornful dancing lady dressed/In black at last reveals/She really isn't there at all," and "When the visions fade—you'll be there/Laying in my tears" are typical lines. They are much more redolent of Brian's genteel, upper-middle-class upbringing than of his reputation as the Stone who outdrank, outfucked and

later outdrugged all the others.

As the Stones slogged through one tour after another—they toured the U.S. alone five times between June 1964 and July 1966—Brian began drinking more heavily, often by himself, in secret. Soon Brian had a new drug—acid—which he then began consuming as profligately as everything else. "Brian was the kind of person who would take anything you gave him" recalled Brion Gysin, a painter and writer who met the Stones in Tangier in 1967. "Offer him a handful of pills, uppers and downers, acid, whatever, and he'd just swallow them all."

Brian could tell himself that the Stones were still his band, and that they would remain his band, until "Satisfaction" made them the Beatles' only serious rivals. But "Satisfaction," which finally turned the band's barbed blues and country-tinged rock and their rebellious, nose-thumbing stance into extremely bankable commodities, was Mick and Keith's show all the way; Brian had virtually nothing to do with it. During the next four years, from the release of "Satisfaction" until he left the band in 1969, Brian would attempt to compensate for Mick and Keith's increasingly tight hammerlock

Keith and Bill at the Between the Buttons *sessions at Olympic Studios in London, late 1966. Overleaf: Andrew Oldham at the Olympic console, producing his last album for the proteges who soon outpaced him.*

on the group's music and image by living that image to the hilt.

After the release of *Out of Our Heads*, their third English studio album and their fourth in America (where it preceded *December's Children*), the Stones no longer had to depend on American blues and soul originals for album material. By this time, they understood perfectly which songs would be right for them and which might misfire, and there were no more disasters.

Both the British and American versions of the albums the Stones made after mid-1965 were strong and consistent; even such occasional clinkers as the anemic soul ballad "That's How Strong My Love Is" were convincing compared to earlier failures. When the Stones rocked, as they did on the Larry Williams screamer "She Said Yeah" or Chuck Berry's pile driver "Talkin' 'bout You," they rocked hard enough to bring back the Fifties. The bleak, emotionally empty Jagger-Richards soul ballad (or antisoul ballad) "Heart of Stone" was strong enough to become a sizable American hit after "Satisfaction." And in "Play with Fire" (the B side of "The Last Time"), "Get Off My Cloud" (single, October 1965), "19th Nervous Breakdown" (February 1966) and "Paint It Black" (May 1966), Mick and Keith began to create a whole world of their own, a world peopled by corrupt debutantes, addled drug abusers in the grip of terminal depression, and average Joes like the narrator of "Get Off My Cloud," who just can't seem to get away from hard-sell commercials, nagging telephone calls, complaining neighbors and the other intrusions into personal space that seem inextricably bound up in the texture of modern life.

Mick and Keith were developing as songwriters at a spectacularly rapid rate. Their first burst of productivity coincided with their decision to share an apartment with Oldham. The arrival of Brian's girlfriend and son from Cheltenham had made some sort of move inevitable, but the two budding tunesmiths and their ambitious young manager grew tighter and tighter during the months they spent living together; this was the real beginning of Brian's alienation from the rest of the group. The Stones' first learning phase, the all-day and all-night blues listening and practice sessions, was over, and Oldham began devoting much of his attention to cultivating the songwriting of his two protégés in the group.

Keith generally handles the music, Mick the words. But not always, which keeps things interesting. This page: Guitar talk with Ian Stewart: The onetime Stone stuck around to be the band's road manager and play piano on their records. But he never forgave Brian for letting Oldham drop him from the stage act.

At first, Oldham had to coax songs out of them, and the results were frequently tepid. But during this early stage, there was no pretense of writing artfully or expressing deep feelings in song. Writing was a commercial proposition, and most of the early Jagger-Richards tunes were banal confections, intended for pop hitmakers like Oldham's buddy Gene Pitney. The Stones would never have considered recording them. But before long, Mick and Keith began writing songs they could show the band without embarrassment. And as they got the hang of collaborating, with Mick tending to handle the words and Keith the music (though there was overlap), Jagger and Richards discovered that they had something to say.

By the time they wrote "Satisfaction," they were saying plenty. After that, each new Stones single was a report from Mick and Keith on the state of the community, that amorphous but by now very self-aware group of hipsters, rockers and more casual fans who bought all the new discs and read them like tea leaves or tarot cards. But unlike many bands of the period, the Stones reported on what they knew and let the chips fall where they may. If the community had to take its lumps along with the adult establishment, so be it. The spoiled society girl who dropped acid in "19th Nervous Breakdown" wasn't using the drug to unlock a psychedelic wonderland, she was simply hastening an already advanced case of mental disintegration. And the dark depression conjured in "Paint It Black" wasn't the sort of side effect drug proselytizers like Timothy Leary talked about when the world was listening. Because the Stones refused to be taken in by any hustle, whether the hustlers were respectable stuffed shirts or street hippies, they earned their audience's trust.

After 1965, Bob Dylan's influence on Mick's lyric writing became increasingly evident. Like a blues singer, Dylan always wrote about himself, no matter how surreal or prolix his imagery. Mick penned a few flowery phrases that were all too reminiscent of Dylan at his wordiest. But in general, Dylan's influence seems to have made Mick more aware of the social and political dimensions of being a pop star. John Lennon fell under Dylan's spell around the same time Mick did, but he didn't start writing songs as outspoken as "Satisfaction" or "Get Off My Cloud." And while Lennon and Dylan himself were using the first-person perspective of the folk tradition to project a self-revealing honesty, the ever mercurial Mick changed perspectives and personas from song to song. Sometimes he was a participant in the events he described; sometimes he was an aloof or even cynical observer. And because his chameleonlike style seemed coolly amoral compared to the more earnest and wholesome Beatles, Mick and the Stones began to be taken somewhat more seriously as revolutionaries by new-left activists and sympathizers. The Beatles, who'd seemed to be so very radical in 1963, were a British national asset by 1965. The mantle of rebellion had fallen squarely on the shoulders of the Stones.

Aftermath, recorded and released in 1966, was the first Stones album to consist entirely of Jagger-Richards originals, and the first to have an impact equal to or greater than the single "Satisfaction." There are fourteen songs on the English version of the album, including "Goin' Home," which at eleven-minutes-plus was then the longest album track in rock history. *Aftermath* caught the Stones at a crucial transitional point, halfway between the blues and soul orientation of earlier days and the more original and organic rock sound that would carry the band through the rest of the Sixties.

Aftermath gives an impression of remarkable diversity, but it's really the resourceful arrangements, and particularly Brian Jones' work on dulcimer, sitar, marimba, harmonica and other

Brian picking up nineteen-year-old German actress Anita Pallenberg at London Airport on December 3, 1966, the day after she'd quit a film set in Munich amid rumors she and Jones were about to marry. Not so, said Brian: "We do not consider that marriage is necessarily the most logical step in our relationship at this time."

In another land: Sir Cecil
Beaton, chronicler of the English
upper crust, captures Keith at
poolside in Morocco. In 1967 and
1968, Keith, Mick and Brian
—plagued by drug busts in
their native England—made
Morocco their second home.

99

High times: a reclining Keith
with Brian, Mick and friend,
Morocco, 1966. Their time in
North Africa had the profound-
est effect on Brian, who discovered there the trance music of the
dervish brotherhoods, and
dreamed of adding exotic new el-
ements to the Stones' sound. In
the end, though, the only tangi-
ble result of this latest musical
passion was Brian Jones Presents
the Pipes of Pan at Jajouka, an
album released after his death.
Overleaf: Keith smoking a sebsi,
sipping mint tea and daydream-
ing at the Kiel Cafe in Tangier,
1966. It was in Morocco that
Keith offered shelter to Anita
Pallenberg—who'd grown
weary of Brian's irrational abuse
—and Anita threw in her lot
with him. For Brian, her desertion was a crippling blow.

instruments that make "Stupid Girl," "Doncha Bother Me," "Flight 505," "Think" and "Goin' Home"—all songs with blues-based melodies and verse structures—sound so different from one another.

The *Aftermath* sessions at RCA Studios in Hollywood found the Stones perfecting the eccentric but (for them) eminently practical recording procedures that would serve them well from then on. The songs Mick and Keith brought in were often little more than sketches; the entire band would then determine the instrumentation and rhythmic direction for each song. They were willing to try almost any approach, no matter how outlandish it might seem or how long it might take, on the theory that it could lead them to discover the perfect arrangement, sound and feel. Thus, "Paint It Black" (which appears on the American *Aftermath* in place of the English version's "Mother's Little Helper"), with its cheesy roller-rink organ, a Dixieland-ish two-beat ryhthm and percussive electric sitar. Bill Wyman inspired this oddest of Stones arrangements by sitting down at the organ to parody Eric Easton—or so the story goes.

WHEN the Stones returned to America in the summer of 1966 for their fifth U.S. tour, the country had changed dramatically, and so had they. They kept encountering longhaired male fans and marijuana, where before they'd seen crew cuts and beer. Mick, Keith and especially Brian were in the first flush of the infatuation with LSD that was sweeping the rock world and what was beginning to be known as the Underground. The Stones' September 11th appearance on the Ed Sullivan show plainly announced what the band's more committed fans already suspected—a mysterious and evidently

Glimmering: Keith and Mick, in Morocco, minus Brian. Below: Keith out on the town with his newly acquired girlfriend, Anita Pallenberg.

profound transformation had over-taken them. On their previous Sullivan appearance, taped only a few months earlier, they had played things rela-tively straight, though Mick's hip-wig-gling drew some protests. But the September Sullivan show could have been staged by Antonin Artaud. Mick's foppish clothes and shoulder-length hair were shockingly androgy-nous, and he minced and flounced around the stage, stopping every now and then to zap the cameras with a leer that suggested borderline psychosis. Brian, festooned with lace, baggy-eyed and haunted, plucked at his dulcimer with a demented flourish during "Lady Jane." The others looked more reason-able, but just barely.

Was this perverse playacting the re-sult of drugs or evidence of serious mental imbalance? Nobody seemed to know for sure. Ed Sullivan was re-volted, especially after the Stones camped through the bizarre "Lady Jane." This band was no longer enter-taining, and parents from coast to coast snapped off their television sets. This band was decadent, evil. Sullivan, who had vowed after their first appearance that the Stones would never be seen on his show again, had to eat those words soon enough; the band returned to the Sullivan show several more times.

But even fans who remained loyal to the Stones and who found the weird-ness of the Sullivan broadcast strange-ly compelling, even liberating, had to think twice about the words to songs like "Under My Thumb." Mick had written it about the English debutante types he was meeting now that he was the toast of London night life. But the class angle was lost on most Ameri-cans, who heard only the song's vicious misogyny.

The hatred of women that seemed so central to the Stones' world view was soon overshadowed, at least for the time being, by broader issues. The Stones and their audience were both beginning to realize that an entire gen-eration of teenagers and young adults was coming of age, a generation that sensed a cultural and maybe a political revolution in the wind and dared to thumb its collective nose at the forces of authority, mostly because the Stones, the Beatles and a few other rock performers seemed willing to be powerful allies, even leaders. Out of this still-amorphous but rapidly swell-ing international movement, a minor-ity—basically the smarter kids, the more reckless ones and the slightly older ones with some sort of roots in earlier, beatnik-era bohemianism—had already made a critical distinction. The Beatles were playing it both ways, trumpeting new attitudes toward sex and drugs in their lyrics while continu-ing to shake their mop tops and flash their cutesy smiles for the teenybop-pers and the moms. The Stones, how-ever, weren't playing the same game.

Mick always told interviewers, whether they were from the daily press or the fan magazines, that he believed teenagers should make up their own minds about sex and drugs and life-styles. He was always careful not to proselytize for sexual or chemical free-dom in his public statements or his lyr-ics. But Stones singles and their albums post-*Aftermath* did comment frankly (and often insightfully) on what was going on. Most of the guardians of pub-lic morals chose to interpret any drug reference in a Number One hit as an endorsement of drug-taking, even if the song carried an essentially antidrug message, as did "19th Nervous Break-down" and "Mother's Little Helper." The Beatles could be tolerated, at least for the time being; the Stones could not. As more and more of the most outspoken young rebels flocked to hear the Stones and to buy their records, the opposition—churchgoers, civic lead-ers, concerned parents—grew more de-termined to stop them or at least teach them and their fans a lesson they would not soon forget.

The Stones' September 1966 Ed Sul-livan appearance was the first of two flagrant gestures that encouraged their

Mick with Marianne Faithfull, the woman found wearing only a fur rug when police raided Keith's Redlands house on the night of February 12, 1967. Asked at the ensuing trial if he thought a woman wearing only a fur rug was "quite normal," Keith replied for the rock ages: "We are not old men. We are not worried about petty morals."

Marianne and Nicholas,
her son by ex-husband John
Dunbar. "I slept with
three of them," she said of
her convergence with the Stones,
"and decided the singer was the
best bet."

Preceding page: Keith with his famous Bentley—the car he bought before he even learned to drive, and proceeded to abuse accordingly—around the time of the Redlands bust. When he crashed the car in 1976, police found cocaine hidden in his jewelry. Left: The Stones as masters of their myth in 1967—with Brian Jones already drifting away.

followers to grow bolder. The second was the release later that month of "Have You Seen Your Mother, Baby, Standing in the Shadow," with its picture sleeve of the band in drag. The music was dense, chaotic, crazed, and recorded on a cheap cassette machine for maximum distortion. The lyrics advised all who took time to decipher them to "take your choice at this time/The brave old world or the slide to the depths of decline." Hard-core Stones fans joyously chose the decline, reasoning that the destruction of civilization as we know it would yield something freer and better. But radio programmers were beginning to feel pressure from above, and even some fans who had followed the Stones this far without a second thought stopped to reconsider. "Mother" made it into the British and American Top Ten on the strength of the Stones' reputation, but it didn't get nearly the radio play that even their most controversial singles had routinely enjoyed, and in Great Britain it was their first single since "Not Fade Away" that failed to reach Number One—a warning sign, if only the Stones had been able to read it, that the counterrevolution had already begun.

The Stones ran into more resistance early in 1967, when their next single, "Let's Spend the Night Together," was censored by several American radio stations, and Jagger was forced to compromise with a panicky Ed Sullivan by singing "let's spend [mumblemumble] together" for the television audience. *Between the Buttons*, released just days later, dropped at least one clue (in Keith's "Connection") that marijuana and psychedelics weren't the only drugs floating around in the Stones' camp. "My bags they get a very close inspection/ I wonder why it is they suspect us," went the last verse. "They're dying to add me to their collection/ And I don't know if they'll let me go."

Although it was recorded on the run and lacked *Aftermath*'s unity of style

I'm sorry girl but I can't stay
Feeling like I do to-day
Staying here is too much
    sorrow
Guess I'll feel the same
    tomorrow.

Well this could be the last
    time,
This could be the last time,
Maybe the last time,
I don't know,
Oh no.

I've told you once and I've
    told you twice
Someone'll have to pay the
    price,
Here's the chance to change
    your mind,
I'll be gone a long long time.

[THE LAST TIME]

and intent, *Between the Buttons* is still one of the best Stones albums. The arrangements are even more varied and more resourceful than on the previous LP, with Brian adding more stringed instruments as well as flutes, recorders and other winds to his arsenal, Keith continuing to perfect his eloquently basic rhythm chording and pungent, twangy leads, and Mick offsetting the vituperative snarl of "All Sold Out" (which complained, "There's not much left to attack") with the melodious sweetness of "Back Street Girl" (English LP) and "Ruby Tuesday" (American LP). But the real antidote to the raving misogyny of earlier Stones diatribes like "Under My Thumb," and *Buttons*' only marginally less abrasive "Yesterday's Papers," wasn't the ballads. It was the women sketched in "She Smiled Sweetly" (the

Jones alone. "Brian was the kind of person who would take anything you gave him," recalled the writer Brion Gysin. "Offer him a handful of pills, uppers and downers, acid, whatever, and he'd just swallow them all."

Ladies and gentlemen, the Rolling Stones. Overleaf: the Redlands raid. Keith was charged with allowing cannabis to be smoked in his house, Mick with possession of four amphetamine tablets. A set-up was heavily suspected in the Stones camp. Said Keith: "The lawyers were saying, 'It seems weird, they want to really do it to you.' "

STONES: 'A STRONG, SWEET SMELL OF INCENSE'

Robert Fraser and Mick Jagger try to shield their faces from photographers on their way to court today.

Story of girl in a fur-skin rug

BY A SPECIAL CORRESPONDENT
Chichester, Sussex, Wednesday

ONE of the party guests at Rolling Stone Keith Richard's house, when it was raided by police one night last February was a young woman wearing only a fur-skin rug, the West Sussex Quarter Sessions jury heard today.

The agony of seeing your idols jailed...

Four of the Rolling Stones at Chichester today before the hearing.

REDLANDS, THE HOUSE IN WHICH POLICE SAID THEY FOUND DRUGS

Tudor-style farmhouse in West Wittering.

KEITH RICHARD
Party pants

Incense found

Rolling Stone Brian remanded

Keith Richard ... after being remanded on bail

ROBERT FRASER
Runs a gallery

Black suit

WHITE TABLETS

SPECIAL JASMINE

'TABLETS WERE FOUND IN A GREEN JACKET'

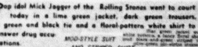

Pop idol Mick Jagger of the Rolling Stones went to court today in a lime green jacket, dark green trousers, a green and black tie and a floral-pattern white shirt to answer drug accusations.

MOD-STYLE SUIT AND STRIPED SHIRT

A green jacket

Art man's sentence to stand

REGINA v. FRASER

The Swinging City

GREEN JACKET
CHANGE OVER

In pipe

NEWS SUMMARY

Jones (of the Stones) on drug charge

2 Stones for trial

MICK JAGGER, lead singer in the Rolling Stones pop group, arrived at a court yesterday in a blue Bentley. He left last night in a grey van—bound with other men on remand to spend a night in Lewes Jail, Sussex.

Green capsules BROWN SUBSTANCE

JAGGER APPEAL
'Wish him luck'

Stones: switch on way to court

MICK JAGGER

KEITH RICHARD   KEITH RICHARD

WOODEN PIPE

Plastic Phial

Italian writing

From Milan

Meal in a cell for Mick Jagger

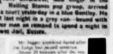

SWINGEING LONDON 1967

supportive type and a friend for life), "Miss Amanda Jones" (dizzy, in a whirl, overprivileged, but she's going to turn out all right) and especially "Complicated" (like the heroine of the later "Memory Motel," this woman's got a mind of her own, and she uses it well).

Mick's attitudes toward women probably hadn't changed that much, but the *range* of his attitudes could be seen a bit more clearly. The women spat at contemptuously in "Under My Thumb," cruelly taunted in "Yesterday's Papers" and casually demolished in "Play with Fire" weren't just *any* women, they were members of the British upper crust, debutantes and models and rich spoiled brats—the sort of women the Stones met, and several of the Stones went for, when their pop success first opened doors that had been closed to them because of class differences. By 1966-67, the Stones had learned a little more about separating the genuine from the phony, regardless of pedigree, and met some admirable women as well as more of the jaded ladies immortalized in the earlier songs.

But the storm clouds on the Stones' horizon just kept growing darker. Less than a month after the release of *Between the Buttons*, police showed up toward the end of an idyllic day of acid tripping at Keith's new country home, Redlands. Little evidence was turned up, but the arresting officers duly noted that Mick's latest girlfriend, pop singer Marianne Faithfull, was wearing nothing but a rug. They also confiscated a few of her speed tablets, which Mick gallantly claimed were his. Three months later, on the day Mick and Keith were being charged (the former for the uppers, the latter for allowing the smoking of marijuana in his home), police burst into Brian's London apartment, found small amounts of cannabis, methedrine and cocaine, and busted him. The heat was on.

Given the state of the Western world, the Stones' uncompromising

I can see that you're fifteen
   years old
No, I don't want your I.D.

But it's no hanging matter,
   it's no capital crime.

Bet your mama don't know
   you scratch like that,
Bet she don't know you can
   bite like that.

You say you got a friend,
   she's wilder than you.
Well, why don't you bring
   her upstairs,
If she's so wild, well she can
   join in too.
But it's no hanging matter,
   it's no capital crime.

Oh yeah, you're a strange
   stray cat,
Oh yeah, don't scratch like
   that.
Oh yeah, you're a strange
   stray cat,
Bet your mama don't know
   you bite like that.
I bet she never saw you
   scratch my back.

[STRAY CAT BLUES]

honesty and exposed position as trend setters and their fondness for drugs (a fondness to which Bill and Charlie seemed largely immune), a run-in with the law was probably inevitable. But it was Brian's big mouth that had triggered the Redlands bust. Drunk in a fashionable London pub, the most indiscrete Stone rambled on about taking LSD, though he characteristically claimed to find it less appealing now that the common rabble were using it. He also popped six bennies and flashed a block of hash in an attempt to lure a couple of groupies back to his apartment. One of his most rapt listeners was apparently a reporter for *The News of the World*, a screaming yellow tabloid roughly equivalent to America's *National Enquirer*. Not much of a rock fan, the journalist mistook Brian for Mick, and when his paper printed the lurid details of "Jagger's" involvement with drugs, Mick (the most cautious Stone in public) announced he was suing for libel. The most likely version of what happened next is that the paper began keeping tabs on Mick and friends, learned about a weekend party at Redlands, assumed the presence of drugs and tipped off the cops.

The Redlands incident was one of the most celebrated drug busts of the Sixties, but the sentences and treatment Mick and Keith received at their trial that June were even more sensational. Mick, fined a hundred pounds and sentenced to three months in jail for a handful of pep pills, and Keith, fined 500 pounds and sentenced to a year in jail simply for allowing pot smoking on his premises, both spent a night in jail. Countless teenagers and college students have experienced

being locked up overnight for drunk driving or some other sort of exuberance. But Mick and Keith didn't have to be overly paranoid to sense the forces of law and order conspiring against them. Were their jailers *really* going to turn them loose? For the first time in their meteoric career, they felt helpless. And after that, things were never quite the same again. The experience radicalized them more thoroughly than any amount of drugs could have. And overnight, they won the sympathy of a large and influential segment of Britain's adult population. The *London Times* cleared its editorial phlegm and asked rhetorically, "Who breaks a butterfly on a wheel?"

A month later, a higher court overturned Keith's sentence and gave Mick a warning and a conditional discharge. The authorities, sympathetic and otherwise, also provided Mick and Keith with a stage and a spotlight, enabling them to speak to many more people than even their records and television appearances had reached. And while Mick was suitably eloquent, if generally circumspect, Keith rose to the occasion with real panache. After gamely allowing a bumbling prosecutor at the initial trial to steer his testimony into the nebulous realm of propriety, partic-

Keith gearing up for the Satanic Majesties *cover-photo session and Mick acting devilish. An ominous time: Richards and Pallenberg were drifting into magic and witchcraft, and Jagger seemed subtly warped by his endless success. The endless drugs only made matters weirder.*

ularly the propriety of Marianne ("Miss X" to the public at large) and her rug, Richards fixed his inquisitor eye to eye and said deliberately, "We are not old men. We are not worried about petty morals." With those words, Keith Richards became the Outlaw Prince of Rock & Roll.

Despite these victories, the Stones could not deny that the busts had taken their toll. Seven months elapsed between the appearance of "Let's Spend the Night Together" and the Stones' next single, "We Love You," which featured a show of solidarity from backing vocalists Lennon and McCartney—along with the sound of a jail door clanging shut, which gave the song's Gandhi-esque sentiments ("We don't care if you hound we . . . you will never love we . . . we love you") a rather ironic edge. By the time "We Love You" was released, in August, Brian had been hospitalized for the first but not the last time following a nervous collapse. In October, he was sentenced to nine months for possession of cannabis. The sentence was set aside that December, but by then his personality had begun to disintegrate. Shortly after the release of "We Love You," Mick and Marianne, in an attempt to get off the drug roller coaster,

traipsed off to North Wales to study Transcendental Meditation with Maharishi Mahesh Yogi. But they soon returned to London, where they drifted back into their normal lifestyles.

To make a shaky situation even worse, Mick, Keith and Brian, the Stones' creative nucleus, were quarreling over musical direction. Along with the arrival of LSD in the summer of 1967 came psychedelic music, which could sound like the universe divulging its most profound secrets if you were tripping, or like self-indulgent noodling if you were straight. Not even the Stones were immune to the spirit of 1967. Mick immersed himself in the esoteric texts that were making the rounds—*The Tibetan Book of the Dead,* the Taoist *Secret of the Golden Flower,* books on C. G. Jung and flying saucers and Atlantis. The Beatles and the Stones had long been running neck and neck on the charts and in the press, but that spring the Moptops had released *Sgt. Pepper's Lonely Hearts Club Band,* a daring departure that hasn't worn very well but exploded like a bombshell at the time, focusing unprecedented attention on rock in general and on the Beatles in particular. The Stones, ever a competitive bunch, reacted as if the Liverpudlians had

Preceding pages: In Rock Dreams, Belgian artist Guy Peellaert envisioned the worst of all possible worlds. Left: Pandancing in a New York hotel room, circa 1967. This page: Brian airing his sinuses at the Monterey Pop Festival in 1967. Hendrix seems to have dropped his.

thrown down the gauntlet, which of course they had. Brian at first resisted the open-ended, improvisational direction the Stones' new music was taking, but Mick argued passionately that it was necessary for the band to expand its musical horizons. In the end, Brian contributed some of the most impressive sounds and effects to the album, which was released in the fall with a lavish three-dimensional picture cover as *Their Satanic Majesties Request.*

Though the album is remembered as an utter catastrophe, it holds up surprisingly well. Consistent it isn't. The lengthy instrumental jam that concludes the first side makes it painfully obvious that none of the Stones was an accomplished improviser. Keith gets in some tangy guitar licks, but nobody manages to really develop anything. Some of the songs work spectacularly, though not in ways one might have expected. "2000 Man" is basically metallic, hopped-up country-western music, an early indication of Keith's longstanding love affair with honky-tonk shitkicking. And while other rock bands were buying in to the proposition that nobody over thirty should be trusted and the certainty that with acid and enlightenment, peace and love, the kids were going to save the planet, the Stones held on to their healthy cynicism. "2000 Man" dared to predict the Aquarian Age's only possible denouement: sooner or later, 1967's hippie utopians were bound to "come down crashing/Seeing all the things you done," having failed to change the world for the better. "It's a big put-on," their children would chide them, and they would respond like every other generation of parents: "My kids, they just don't understand me at all."

"Citadel," "The Lantern" and "2000 Light Years from Home" almost offhandedly created classical rock clichés that arena bands like Emerson, Lake and Palmer, Yes and the Electric Light Orchestra would spend much of the Seventies refining into schtick,

Oh, the singer looks so angry
At being thrown to the
    lions,
And the bass player looks so
    nervous
About the girls outside,
And the drummer he was
    shattered
Trying to keep on time,
And the guitar player looks
    damaged
They've been outcasts all
    their lives.

Me, I'm waiting so patiently
    lying on the floor,
I'm just tryin' to do my
    jigsaw puzzle
Before it rains any more.

[JIGSAW PUZZLE]

though none of these bands would ever create anything quite as otherworldly as Brian's Mellotron parts or the shimmering electronic and vocal textures on Bill Wyman's "In Another Land." This music retained at least a few shreds of the Stones' grounding in American roots music as well as a firm commitment to concise pop-song structures.

Mick, for one, is still fond of *Their Satanic Majesties Request.* It's dated more than other Stones music, with the possible exception of some of the early cover tunes and the most turgid moments on mid-Seventies albums like *Goat's Head Soup.* But pop music should be true to its time even as it transcends it, and in 1967, behind a hit of Owsley acid, *Satanic Majesties* was an unqualified success.

It is a minor miracle that *Satanic Majesties* holds up at all, considering the circumstances of its creation. Mick

Mick clutching lyrics during the Beggar's Banquet *sessions at Olympic Studios, sometime between March and June 1968. Overleaf: Mick and Keith, deeply into their roles, with Brian, slumped at bottom right, deteriorating fast. It was to be the last full Stones album for Jones, the man who "simply transcended addiction as we know it."*

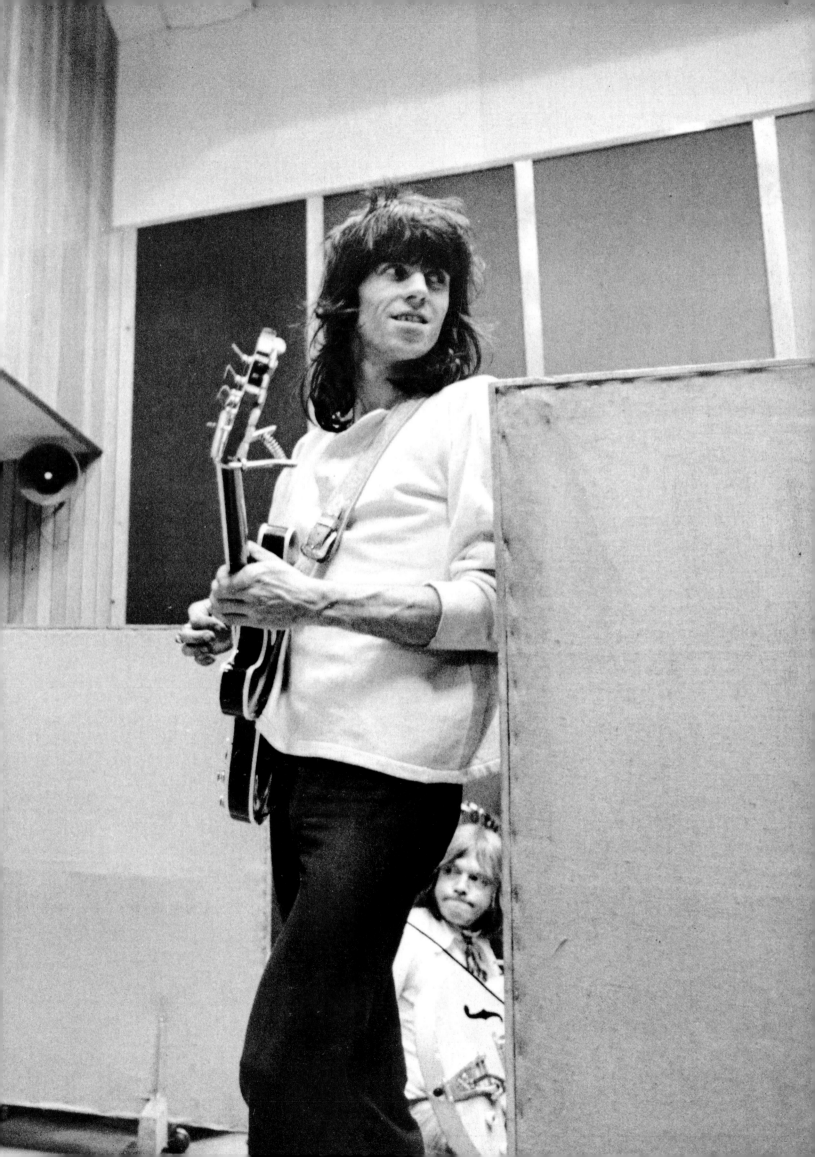

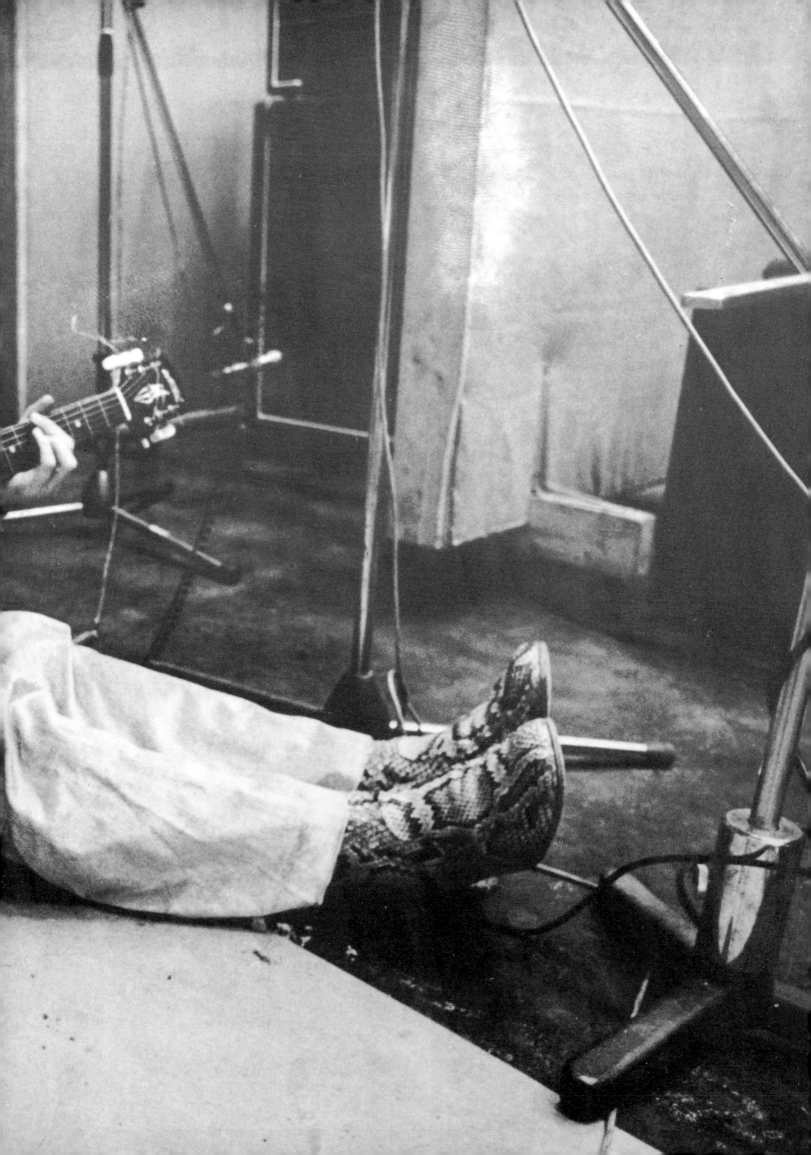

and Keith went to trial, went to jail, were convicted and then succeeded in overturning their convictions while it was being recorded. In the midst of their troubles with the law, they were dissolving their business partnership with Oldham. As their celebrity outstripped his image-making, he began to seem more and more manipulative, and besides, they felt, he was pocketing too much of their earnings. Keith and Mick hadn't lived with him for a while by this time. They had grown away from him, and they'd grown up enough to confidently take charge of their own record production and business affairs. The takeover of the Stones by the Glimmer Twins was now complete.

Meanwhile, Brian was going to pieces. By the end of 1967, he had suffered another nervous collapse, and his behavior and performance in the studio were becoming increasingly erratic. Playing guitar parts with Keith no longer interested him much, especially since Keith was writing most of the band's music and usually had very specific ideas about what the guitars should be doing. Mick and Keith recorded several of the tracks on *Satanic Majesties*, as well as most of the singles and album tracks of the next two years, on their own. It was only when the tracks were almost finished that they called in Brian and let him add musical seasoning, using whatever instruments struck his fancy. At times, he was lucid and brilliant. At other times, he was too wrecked to play a note.

My bags they get a very
      close inspection.
I wonder why it is that they
      suspect us,
They're dying to add me to
      their collection
And I don't know if they'll
      let me go.

Connection, I just can't
      make no connection,
But all I want to do is to get
      back to you.
Connection, I just can't
      make no connection,
But all I want to do is get
      back to you.

[CONNECTION]

their ascension to pop demigod status. But they also knew that as long as they stayed in England, there would always be the threat of another bust. The police raided Brian's London apartment again in May 1968, and once again he was charged with possession of cannabis. The pressure was still mounting, and Morocco, where European decadents had long ago found they could escape civilization's moral constraints without having to say goodbye to its conveniences, was the ideal spot.

Morocco was especially important to Brian. There he discovered the trance music of the dervish brotherhoods, and that experience helped him to hear all music in a new way. But his ego suffered a crippling blow when Anita Pallenberg, his ravishingly beautiful girlfriend, decided she'd had enough of his drugged torpors and childish tantrums, nagging insecurity and paranoia. One afternoon during a communal acid trip in Marrakesh, she decided to throw in her lot with Keith.

There were always plenty of women

M OROCCO became a kind of second home for Brian, Keith and Mick during 1967 and 1968. They'd had enough of the touring grind by the end of 1966 and figured it was time to enjoy their wealth and explore some of the ramifications of

to help Brian salve his wounds, and the effects of Anita's desertion weren't immediately apparent. Besides, Morocco's trance music intrigued Brian; several of his friends have suggested that he was never happier than when he was taping the insistent rhythms of the G'naoua and the Mejdoubi brotherhoods in the great square of Marrakesh. He was particularly attracted to the G'naoua, black Moroccans whose ancestors had been carried north across the Sahara as slaves, from the West African coastal region that was suffering the depredations of American and English slavers around the same time. The G'naoua healed the physically sick and cured mental illnesses with their kinetic drumming and the hypnotic clickclack of their iron castanets. When they sang and played their three-stringed lutes, they sounded like primitive Mississippi bluesmen. Here at last was a musical project that Brian could pursue on his own. He decided to tape a G'naoua rhythm track and overdub a black American soul band on top of it, and he began telling sympathetic listeners he intended to add Moroccan trance rhythms to the Stones' music, too. When his G'naoua tapes didn't turn out as well as he'd anticipated, Brion Gysin took him to a village called Jajouka, up in the Rif foothills south of Tangier. There, a family of musicians played an ancient ritual music that was even more powerful than the G'naoua rhythms, and worshipped the goat-god Pan. This time, Brian brought a reliable recording engineer and made plenty of tapes. He was in and out of various studios for months after that, working on the tapes, adding echo and other effects, producing what eventually became his posthumous album, *Brian Jones Presents the Pipes of Pan at Jajouka.*

The experimentation that went into the recording of *Satanic Majesties* and Brian's subsequent immersion in Moroccan music brought the Stones to a decisive crossroads in their musical

Your heart is like a diamond,
You throw your pearls at
   swine,
And as I watched you
   leaving me,
You packed my peace of
   mind.

Our love was like the water
That splashes on a stone,
Our love is like our music
It's here and then it's gone.

So take me to the airport
And put me on a plane,
I've got no expectations
To pass through here again.

[NO EXPECTATIONS]

evolution. Brian, Mick and Keith were divided among themselves, unsure which way they should go. The music that mattered most to them was still black American blues, R&B and soul music; the tapes Mick and Keith listened to most frequently on their Moroccan sojourns consisted of singles by Solomon Burke, Don Covay and other soul singers, along with Otis Redding's *The Soul Album.* But Mick and Keith were gradually moving away from traditional blues and soul song forms. Brian, often the most original and almost always the most unpredictable musician in the band, was also the one who kept complaining that the songs Mick and Keith were writing were taking the Stones too far from their blues roots. He loved the Stones' supercharged rock & roll for its powerful effect on audiences, but he loved the pained cry at the heart of the blues as much or more.

Brian enjoyed talking about revamping the Stones' music, using G'naoua and Jajouka trance rhythms as a new foundation and combining Arabic prayer-call melodies with blues and gospel shadings. He might well have been capable of pulling off such a fusion; his winding Mellotron melody on "We Love You" is particularly convincing evidence. Had he somehow regained his health and his mental equilibrium and convinced the other Stones to help him put his ideas into practice in the studio, the results might have sent all rock spinning off in a startling new direction. But without the rest of the band, most of his ideas were bound to remain unrealized. He was an original musician in his way, but he seemed unable to establish a setting or context for his own best work. For that, he depended on the other Stones. Unfortunately, after he returned to London, he again fell in with the party crowd, and his dreams were quickly forgotten.

When the Stones returned to the studio in the spring of 1968, they had hired a new producer, Jimmy Miller, a young American hotshot who had been making crisp, punchy records with Traffic. And they had a new batch of Jagger-Richards songs, including "Jumpin' Jack Flash," "Sympathy for the Devil" and "Street Fighting

Man." These were great rock & roll songs, some of the Stones' all-time best. But they weren't Moroccan trance-and-roll, and Brian's only contribution to them consisted of a few sparkling solos, overdubbed on tracks that otherwise were shaped entirely by Mick and Keith.

The band's squabble with Decca over the photo of the graffiti-covered urinal they wanted on the cover held up *Beggar's Banquet* for several months. When the album was finally released in December, with a plain white cover, it received careful scrutiny in publications that hadn't even existed when the Stones were a touring band, publications that were taking rock *and* rock criticism seriously. *Crawdaddy* had been the first, followed by *Rolling Stone*, which trumpeted *Beggar's Banquet* as a "Rolling Stones comeback."

Beggar's Banquet, possibly the greatest of all Stones albums, and certainly among their top two or three, was everything the critics claimed and a great deal more besides. It captured the Stones at their most explosive ("Sympathy for the Devil," "Street Fighting Man") and their most soulful ("No Expectations" and the lovely Robert

Once more, for old time's sake: Mick and Keith with Brian at Keith's cottage in 1969. In June, the Stones told Brian he was out of the group.

The Stones hold a press confer-
ence on June 8 to introduce Brian's replacement: guitar virtuoso
Mick Taylor, formerly of John
Mayall's Bluesbreakers. It was
the end of the Stones' dual-gui-
tar attack, and the beginning of
a more standard lead-and-
rhythm approach.

145

Wilkins country-gospel tune "Prodigal Son"). It was the first Stones album since the band stopped covering soul and R&B tunes to feature a song not written by any of the Stones, though its final cover listed Jagger and Richards as the authors of "Prodigal Son," anyway, and Wilkins, still playing bluesy slide guitar and preaching in Memphis, had to pester the Stones to get his royalties. But this temporary hitch didn't deter the band, and more particularly Keith, from making sure there was a country-blues or old-time gospel song on most of the later albums. "For a couple of years there," Keith has recalled, "I couldn't listen to much besides Fred McDowell or Robert Johnson records."

But throughout *Beggar's Banquet*, the most ravishing slide-guitar playing was Brian's. His glancing, ghostly phrasing on "No Expectations" was perhaps his most transcendent moment, and his solos on "Parachute Woman" and "Jigsaw Puzzle" suffered only by comparison. Brian had somehow overcome the drugs and depression and come up with a fresh slant on slide guitar. His work on *Beggar's Banquet* did not sound remotely like that of any other musician, black or white, living or dead. In black folk culture, slide playing has always followed the

Brian Jones was found dead in his swimming pool on July 3, 1969. The coroner's verdict: death by misadventure. Overleaf: Brian's parents, Mr. and Mrs. Lewis Jones, and Suki Potier, the last of his many girlfriends, at Brian's funeral in Cheltenham on July 10, 1969. The rector read from a letter Brian had written to his parents before his death: "Please don't judge me too harshly," he'd asked. Said Pete Townshend: "It's a normal day for Brian, like he died every day, you know."

contours of speech or singing, and Brian's slide on *Beggar's Banquet* spoke volumes. He must have outdone himself on "No Expectations" because the song's story was *his* story, the feelings his feelings as he could never have expressed them himself:

> *. . . as I watched you leaving me*
> *You packed my peace of mind . . . .*
> *So take me to the airport*
> *And put me on the plane,*
> *I've got no expectations*
> *To pass through here again.*

THE title the Stones chose for their psychedelic album, *Their Satanic Majesties Request*, led to speculation that the band's guiding lights were dabbling in Satanism, if not actively in league with Lucifer. The title was actually a pun on words found in every English passport, "Her Brittanic Majesty Requests," but a little black magic and Satanism stirred up a lot of controversy, and the more people talked, the more interested in the subject Mick and Keith became.

Mick's interest was primarily, perhaps entirely, intellectual, as his lyrics to "Sympathy for the Devil," *Beggar's Banquet*'s most talked-about track, clearly indicated. Mick was well-read, and he made the song's imagery rich enough to support the wildest intellectual glosses without losing its power. It seems likely that more farfetched philosophical exegeses have been constructed around this song than around any other rock composition. But there was beginning to be more behind the Stones' evil image than abstract ideas and clever wordplay. Mick's ambition and his upward-spiraling success were subtly warping him; associates noticed that he was becoming more and more wrapped up in his own thoughts and

I've got nasty habits
I take tea at three
Yes, and the meat I eat for
   dinner
Must be hung up for a week.
My best friend he shoots
   water rats
And feeds them to his geese,
Doncha think there's a place
   for you in between the
   sheets?
Come on now, honey, we
   can build a home for
   three.
Come on now, honey, don't
   you want to live with me?

[LIVE WITH ME]

image. Bill and Charlie attempted to puncture his inflated ego and his absorption in role playing with well-aimed darts, only to find that Mick was so caught up in the personas he had developed, he couldn't tell with any certainty where roles ended and his "real" personality began. Meanwhile, Keith and Anita were dabbling in magic rituals and witchcraft. And everywhere Mick—and especially Keith and Anita—turned, there were drugs, drugs, drugs. When they encountered a sensitive soul—an engineer, say, or a photographer who suddenly began spending hours in their company— Mick and Keith were a dangerous and potentially deadly influence, and too wrapped up in their own interior processes to really notice. There were burnouts around them, and deaths from drug overdoses, and yet they themselves seemed to emerge unscathed. *Were* they the Devil in disguise? And if so, did they really deserve sympathy?

"Sympathy for the Devil" kicked off *Beggar's Banquet* with a frontal assault

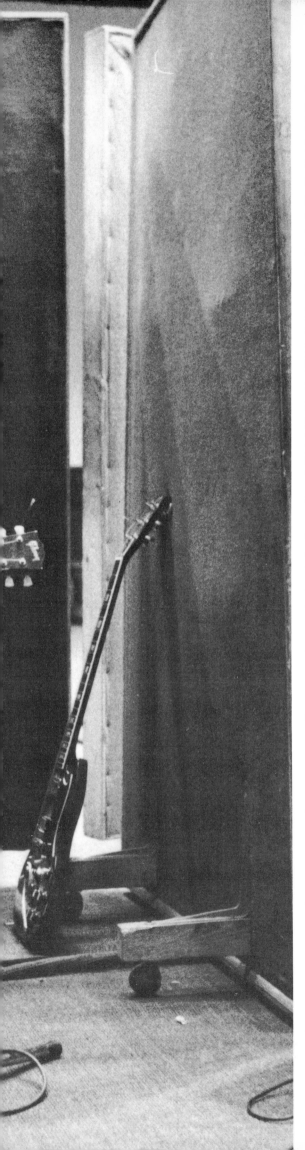

on conventional values, and the attack continued in songs like "Stray Cat Blues" ("I can see that you're fifteen years old . . . but it's no hanging matter, it's no capital crime. . . . Bet your mama don't know you bite like that"), "Jigsaw Puzzle" (ingenious, self-referential image-making, with "angry" Mick, "damaged" Keith, even "shattered" Charlie thumbing their noses at polite society, "outcasts all their lives") and "Street Fighting Man," which was jerry-built layer by layer on top of a deliberately crude, cassette-recorded rhythm track. "Street Fighting Man" bothered so many people, they failed to notice that, while the Stones smelled revolution in the air, they weren't signing up for it: "What can a poor boy do/ Except to sing for a rock and roll band/'Cause in sleepy London town/ There's just no place for a street fighting man."

Despite some defections because of suspicions of Satanism, *Beggar's Banquet* delighted most of the Stones' older fans, and it won the band some new ones. Mick, Keith, Bill and Charlie were eager to tour again, but Brian had neither the physical nor the mental stamina to go on the road, and everyone in the Stones camp knew it. So the Stones and some guests—John Lennon, Eric Clapton, Pete Townshend and various circus freaks—filmed a special for British television, "The Rolling Stones' Rock and Roll Circus." Brian looked wasted and lost and whispered his lines, Keith was distant, and on the whole, the show was a rambling indulgence; it was shown to mixed reviews in England, promised but never shown in the U.S.

Meanwhile, the external pressures were steadily mounting. In May 1969, Mick and Marianne were busted for possession of hashish. And by then, Brian was taking so many different drugs and drinking such enormous quantities of alcohol that he simply transcended addiction as we know it. The band's enemies, especially establishment types, were watching.

Recording Let It Bleed: *Mick Taylor (left) took Brian's place in the band, but was never really one of the boys.*

Please allow me to introduce
myself
I'm a man of wealth and
taste.
I've been around for many a
long, long year
I've stolen many a man's
soul and faith.

I was around when Jesus
Christ had His moments
of doubt and pain,
I made damn sure that Pilate
washed his hands and
sealed his fate.

Pleased to meet you, hope
you guess my name,
But what's puzzling you, is
the nature of my game.

[SYMPATHY FOR THE DEVIL]

Mick, Keith and Charlie paid Brian a visit in early June, told him they felt the Stones had to tour and graciously accepted his resignation. Then they left him to the wolves—the spongers and hangers-on who seemed to always surround Brian and were now staying with him for days on end at his country home, taking his drugs and drinking his liquor. Some of his old friends, including blues guitarist Alexis Korner, visited him during the next few weeks to offer encouragement or just to talk about music and life. But a month after his departure from the Rolling Stones was made public, Brian was found dead in his swimming pool. The cause of death was accidental drowning associated with the consumption of alcohol and barbiturates.

The day after the funeral, Decca released a new Stones single that was a study in basics. One side, "Honky Tonk Women," was built on one of Keith's simplest, most durable guitar riffs; the other, "You Can't Always Get What You Want," on the most basic of chord sequences, I-IV-I-IV and so on. "Honky Tonk Women" remains the Stones' great drinking song, and its guitar riff, which Keith often plays with one hand on his open-tuned guitar, has passed into the basic vocabulary of rock & roll. "You Can't Always Get What You Want" is basic Stones philosophy. It might be about

On the road again: Riding high with "Honky Tonk Women," and about to unleash their Let It Bleed *album, the Stones flew to Los Angeles in the fall of 1969 and set off on their first U.S. tour in three years. Everything seemed the same—maybe bigger, better—but not for long. This page: backstage with Ike and Tina Turner.*

Preceding page: Hell's Angels at
Altamont. The Stones concluded
their 1969 tour with a free concert at the Altamont Motor
Speedway, near San Francisco.
The mood of the event was ugly
from the outset. Mick Jagger
was punched in the head by a
young fan screaming, "I hate
you. I want to kill you." That
night, during the Stones' set, a
young black man named Meredith
Hunter, who may have been
wielding a pistol, was stabbed to
death by one of the Hell's Angels
the group had hired for security.
Just three and a half months after Woodstock, the "Aquarian
dream" of the Sixties had come
to an end.

drug addiction, about the one lesson every junkie learns: "You can't always get what you want, but if you try sometimes, you just might find you get what you need." The somewhat elliptical references to a connection in the lyrics, and the similarity of the opening I-IV-I-IV chord scheme to the opening chords of Lou Reed's Velvet Underground classic "Heroin," support this contention. But like so many Stones songs, this one also can support a much broader interpretation. The halcyon Sixties had held the promise of getting what one wanted, whether it was drugs or free love or simply the freedom to be what one wanted to be. The Seventies were dawning dark and troubled, for the Stones and for their fans. It would be necessary to come to grips with radically reduced expectations, to forget about casual wanting and get down to basic necessities. You'd better figure out what your real *needs* are and go after *them*, the Stones seemed to be saying, and even that might not be so easy: "If you *try* sometimes, you *might* find you get what you need." This was a message worth heeding. But for Brian Jones, rainbow-chasing child of the Sixties, it came too late.

T HE Stones seemed to bounce back from Brian Jones' death remarkably quickly—much too quickly for some Stones-watchers, who imagined all sorts of sinister conspiracies. For by 1969, the band was playing such a potent, active role in so many people's fantasies that believing Brian had simply popped too many pills and accidentally drowned in his swimming pool required as great a leap of faith as believing he had been murdered by Mick and Keith or by the Mafia, or overcome by supernatural forces he had called up but could not control.

Surely nothing about the Stones could be as simple, as much a plain, tawdry waste, as Brian's death seemed to be. But the surviving Stones knew it was exactly that. They were able to go on with their plans for a free concert in Hyde Park on July 5 and to introduce a new guitarist, Mick Taylor.

At the concert, Mick read from Shelley's "Adonais" and released hundreds of butterflies as a eulogy to Brian. And the band plowed through its set with a professionalism worthy of its newest addition, a blues-based guitar virtuoso whose lyrical lead lines and solos seemed to pour from his amp like honey. That the Stones had gone ahead with the show was considered by some to be in poor taste, but a film of the event, made for English television, shows a band too overwhelmed by lethargy and confusion to be tasteless. Mick looked nervous, drawn and decidedly uncomfortable in an odd, knee-length white smock. The cameras avoided Keith so successfully that he was seen only for a few seconds, and then at a distance, and Mick Taylor stood rooted to one spot, playing cleanly and cautiously. Even Bill and Charlie sounded and looked beat.

The Stones had started recording songs for their next album more than a month before Brian's death. They worked primarily as a four-piece band, with Keith putting down all the guitar parts and Jagger's harmonica providing an additional instrumental voice. By the time the Stones arrived in America in the fall, they were able to kick off their first U.S. tour since 1966 looking and sounding like conquering heroes. Keith, now the band's undisputed musical center and the key to its continuing evolution, decided to concentrate on further sharpening his skills as a rhythm guitarist and to take advantage of Mick Taylor's fluid, graceful lyricism and flair for melodic invention by giving him most of the solo spots and leads. The Stones paid Brian the highest compliment by not even attempting to replace him. For the next five years,

The Rolling Stones in the early Seventies.

Yeah, we all need someone
   we can dream on,
And if you want it, well you
   can dream on me.
Yeah, we all need someone
   we can cream on,
And if you want to, well you
   can cream on me.

I was dreaming of a steel
   guitar engagement
When you drank my health
   in scented jasmine tea,
You knifed me in my dirty
   filthy basement
With that jaded faded junky
   nurse, oh what pleasant
   company.

We all need someone we can
   feed on,
And if you want it, well you
   can feed on me.
Take my arm, take my leg
Oh, baby, don't you take my
   head.

[LET IT BLEED]

the Stones would build their songs around precise, streamlined guitar arrangements that usually made a clear and relatively conventional distinction between lead and rhythm parts, in sharp contrast to the more integrated two-guitar work of their early years.

Let It Bleed hit the streets just before the Stones tour hit New York City. During the tour's earlier dates, they had tightened the new lineup while retaining the spirit and the edge that Mick Taylor's arrival had generated. Their shows at New York's Madison Square Garden were even more mag-

Mick got some good reviews for his portrayal of a drugged-out pop star in the 1971 Nicolas Roeg film, Performance, *in which he starred with Anita Pallenberg and British actor James Fox. But the aura of decadence that hung about the Stones followed him onto the film set. Fox became so fascinated by the sensual, amoral world that Mick and Anita appeared to rule that he began taking drugs and suffered a nervous breakdown before finally finding religion. He wasn't the first Stones associate to burn out attempting to keep up the pace, and he wouldn't be the last.*

170

By the spring of 1971, the Stones had grown too wealthy to remain in tax-heavy England. Mick, Keith and Bill decamped for the south of France, and with their departure, swinging London, go-go capital of the Western world, passed into history. Jagger marked the end of the age on May 12, in St. Tropez, where he married Nicaraguan socialite Bianca Perez Moreno de Macias. Mick's new image—social butterfly and talk-of-the-town celebrity —appalled many Stones fans.

nificent than *Get Yer Ya-Ya's Out*, the live album that was drawn from them and released the following year. *Gimme Shelter*, the documentary film the Maysles Brothers made of the trek, doesn't quite capture the tour's intensity, either, dominated as it is by the specter of Altamont.

For a substantial portion of the rock audience, Altamont was the end of a dream that had seemed within their grasp just a few months earlier, in the glow of the good feeling and utopian sentiments that Woodstock had inspired. This idealistic, frequently repeated and widely accepted slant on rock & roll's most eventful six months since the arrival of Elvis Presley and Chuck Berry in 1955 did offer a tidy and therefore comforting explanation for some extremely disturbing events. But it was too tidy, and the events were too complex.

The Stones had asked the Grateful Dead for advice once they decided to cap their tour with a free concert in the San Francisco area. The Dead told them to hire the Hell's Angels for security. The Angels—berserk on speed, psychedelics and beer and besieged by as wigged-out a bunch of fans as ever filled the front rows at a rock show—set up their bikes in the crowd, waited for them to be overturned and then retaliated by beating people indiscriminately and stabbing one man, Meredith Hunter, to death.

The Stones must have realized almost as soon as they arrived at the speedway that they had made a terrible mistake. The Jefferson Airplane's Marty Balin had been knocked to the ground, out cold, by an irate Angel earlier in the day. Mick stepped out the door of the trailer that served as his dressing room not long after he arrived and someone threw a punch at him. By the time the Stones went on, night had fallen and the atmosphere was ugly and getting uglier. And in the weird, reddish glare, the Stones' music seemed to cast an evil glow of its own—especially "Sympathy for the Devil,"

Well now we're respected in
 society, you ain't worried
 'bout the things that used
 to be.
We're talking heroin with
 the President,
Yes, it's a problem, sir, but it
 can be bent.

Well now you're a pillar of
 society, you're not
 worried about things you
 used to be.
You're a rag-trade girl,
 you're the queen of porn,
You're the easiest lay on the
 White House lawn.
Get out of my life—don't
 come back
Get out of my life—don't
 come back.

[RESPECTABLE]

which unleashed the crowd's hysteria and seemed to beat out a dark tattoo in rhythm with the Angels' blood lust.

The Stones hadn't understood the difference between British and American motorcycle clubs, and they hadn't counted on performing to a crowd that seemed bent on misadventure and mayhem. They could have refused to go on, but that seemed virtually certain to spark a riot and might well have resulted in more injuries and deaths than actually did occur. The band did stop playing several times in an attempt to prevent further bloodshed. But afterward, when all was said and done, it was difficult to shake the creepy feeling that the dark underside of the Stones' power, the voodoo in their rhythms, had suddenly turned on them like a maddened animal.

Charlie at the entrance to Nellcote, Keith's home-in-exile in the South of France. Richards' drug problems and (understandable) legal paranoia made music-making more and more difficult for the far-flung Stones.

Fortunately, the exhilarating music the Stones had made earlier in the tour and captured on *Let It Bleed* endured along with Altamont's evil afterglow. *Let It Bleed* meant many things to many people, but amid the images of war, rape and murder, amid all of life's "hard knox and durty sox," there *were* rays of hope. Shelter, which could be permanent and just a shot away, could also mean salvation and be just a kiss away. These songs, and the others on the album, demanded an intensely personal response. And their message— "all my love's in vain," but "honey, you can bleed on me"—came wrapped in layer upon layer of shimmering guitars, almost all of them played by Keith.

Keith can stake his reputation as one of rock's great guitarists on *Let It Bleed* alone. The menacing welter of guitars on "Gimme Shelter" is all his; so are the seminal rhythm riffs that propel "Midnight Rambler," "Live with Me" and "Monkey Man." And the haunting, ethereal "You Got the Silver," with its delicately interlocking picking and chording and the wailing vocal, is Keith all the way.

But if Stones fans and especially Keith's fans embraced *Let It Bleed* and wrote off Altamont as a stupid tragedy that was nobody's fault but the An-

Keith at Nellcote with Anita, Gram Parsons and Parsons' girlfriend. Gram taught Keith about country soul; Keith taught Gram about nasty habits. Below: Marshall Chess.

Yeah, heard the diesel
    drumming all down the
    line,
Oh, heard the wires
    a-humming all down the
    line,
Yeah, hear the women
    sighing all down the line,
Oh, hear the children crying
    all down the line.

(All down the line)
We'll be watching out for
    trouble, yeah
(All down the line)
And we'd better keep the
    motor running, yeah.
(All down the line)

[ALL DOWN THE LINE]

gels', many others refused to forget so easily. There was violence in the Stones' music and violence at Altamont, and somehow the two seemed inextricably linked. After Altamont was over, the Stones simply had walked away. They were wealthy men, and they had the luxury of that option. But if they thought for an instant that walking away would really be that simple, they were wrong. After Altamont, being a Rolling Stone would never be quite the same. They would carry with them the images of death, the demonic faces in the crowd, the scene in *Gimme Shelter* when Meredith Hunter goes down under the Angels' attack, from then on. In addition, Altamont proved the last straw for a vocal minority of rock fans who had been bothered by the violence and misogyny in the Stones' music for a long time, and who now concluded that their former idols were beneath contempt. The view that the Stones

Preceding photo: Keith and Gram Parsons in back, Anita up front with friends, tooling around Los Angeles. Left: Keith and Mick in L.A. in the early Seventies.

had become rich, jaded decadents who cared more for their drugs and their groupies and their privilege than they did for their fans began gathering momentum. By the mid-Seventies, it would reach overwhelming proportions.

W ITH the Beatles' breakup in 1970, there were few groups left to challenge the Stones' claim as the greatest rock & roll band. Still, rock had always been a young man's game, and after almost a decade in the spotlight, capped by one murder and three accidental deaths at Altamont, the Stones no longer felt young. Over the next few years, well-meaning friends and associates repeatedly asked the same question—could this be the last time?—and they weren't being rhetorical. Keith ignored them, and so did Mick Taylor. Bill and Charlie were living as comfortable country gentlemen when the Stones weren't touring or recording, busying themselves with families and hobbies (Bill's photography and work as the band's historian, Charlie's lifelong study of jazz). As long as the Stones rolled, Bill and Charlie were content to roll along.

By this time, Mick wasn't just a rock & roll singer, he had become an entertainer, a celebrity, a man whose name appeared in gossip columns as often as it did in the music press—*more* often, as the Seventies went on. Mick's next career step obviously had to be films. He cut an impressive figure in Jean-Luc Godard's semidocumentary *Sympathy for the Devil (One Plus One)*, which captured the Stones—including Brian Jones—recording that ostensible anthem. A few days after Brian's death in July 1969, Mick flew to Australia with Marianne to begin filming *Ned Kelly*, a movie abut a historical Down-Under Robin Hood figure, in which Mick played the title role. This was his real acting debut, and he was nervous and self-absorbed. Marianne couldn't seem to break through his protective shell, and Brian's death and the latest busts had left her confused and vulnerable. She swallowed a bottle of pills, hoping for a quick and painless death. Instead, she awoke to find herself in a hospital bed, with Mick at her side. He was attentive and she was penitent, but their romance had almost run its course.

Sympathy for the Devil opened in the U.S. in March 1970, followed by *Ned*

In May 1972, the Stones released Exile on Main Street *and then launched yet another American tour. With such writers as Terry Southern and Truman Capote aboard for the ride, this latest installment of the band's never-ending roadshow was a celebrity circus—a necessary change, perhaps, from the devil-dogged days of 1969. Right: Mick Taylor learns about show business.*

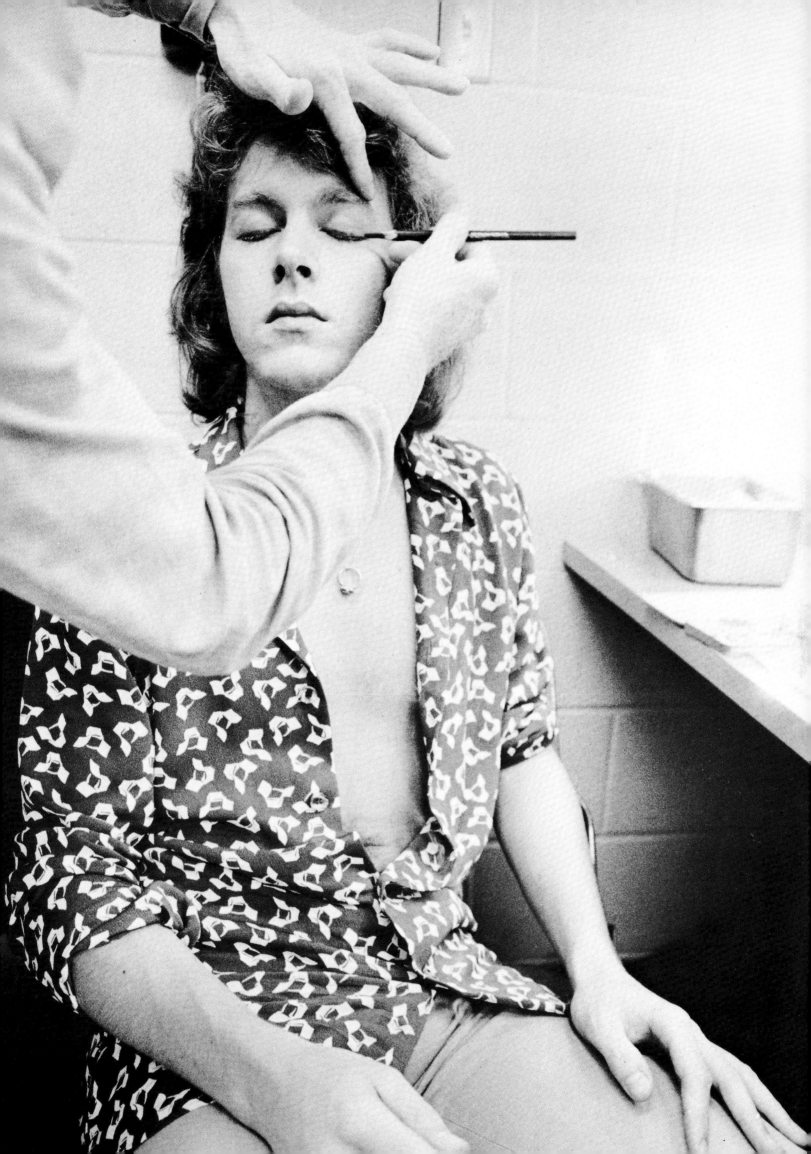

Kelly in October and *Gimme Shelter* in December. Only *Ned Kelly* gave Mick a chance to act, and his portrayal received mixed reviews. The Stones toured Europe in the fall, then took time off while Mick filmed *Performance*, the Donald Cammell-Nicolas Roeg psychological study that drew its central ideas from William Burroughs and much of its power from the Stones' dark mystique. Mick played Turner, a drugged-out pop star who trades identities with a small-time gangster on the run, played by James Fox. Anita Pallenberg played one of Turner's two live-in girlfriends, a luminous beauty with a hint of decay. Fox found Anita and Mick fast company in real life; there apparently were as many drugs on the set as there were in the plot, which hinged on a magic mushroom psychedelic trip that enabled Mick's and Fox' characters to swap identities and fates. Fox, the story goes, became so fascinated by the sensual, amoral world that Mick and Anita appeared to rule with such impressive disdain that he began taking drugs and suffered a nervous breakdown before finally finding religion. He wasn't the first Stones associate to burn out after attempting to keep up the pace, and he wouldn't be the last. For, as Glimmer Twin Keith Richards once remarked, "a touch of glimmer can be more addicting than smack."

Performance cleverly portrayed what many had pictured as the Stones' world—a scene that was at once alluring, decadent, druggy and reeking of death. But the reality was somewhat different. By this time, the Stones had become—like Lucifer of "Sympathy for the Devil"—men of wealth and taste. Mick and Keith had been splitting the songwriting royalties from Stones albums since *Aftermath* and getting richer and richer. By the spring of 1971, they had grown too rich to remain in England, where taxes would have taken more than ninety percent of their earnings. Home and hearth were appealing—perhaps—but not as ap-

pealing as cash. Mick and Keith decided to hold on to as much as they could by joining the ranks of tax exiles. Charlie elected to remain in England, but Wyman followed Mick and Keith to the south of France, and with their departure, swinging London, go-go capital of the Western world, passed into history.

The move was probably inevitable. Mick, especially, was becoming less a citizen of any country than a multinational rock & roll executive, scion of

Even as he approached thirty, Jagger (preceding pages) still seemed at ease with the glitter and the greasepaint of the Stones' stage act: he would keep performing as long as there was an audience for his art. Keith, however, was coming apart. Left: Bill, Stones chronicler, amateur photographer, the very prototype of the reclusive rock bassist. Below: the country gentleman of the group, and drummer extraordinaire.

the Seventies jet set. He underscored that by showing up on a list of the world's One Hundred Best Dressed Men, printed in the snooty *Tailor and Cutter*, before he'd even had a chance to settle into his new French digs. He left Marianne behind when he left England, and, after enjoying himself for a time as one of European high society's most eligible bachelors, he gave his fans a real shock—and confirmed his top-of-the-gossip-column status—by announcing his impending marriage to Bianca Perez Moreno de Macias, actor Michael Caine's ex. The wedding ceremony, held in St. Tropez on May 12, struck a crushing blow to the Stones' rock & roll credibility. Mick failed to realize that most of his fans had bought the image he'd created for himself over the years, the image of the androgynous anarchist-trickster, implacable foe of the establishment. And his new image—the social butterfly and talk-of-the-town celebrity—appalled them. It appalled Keith Richards, too. He registered his own private protest at the wedding by hurling an ashtray through a thick glass window.

Given Mick's restless nature, his fascination with extremes and his determination to carve out a long-term career that would sustain him after he was too old to rock & roll, partying with and even marrying into the Western social elite made perfect sense. But Stones fans who weren't simply grossed out by it were at least mystified. Rock icons had entered into surprising marriages before, but not without attempting to explain themselves. John Lennon had gone out of his way to explain his love for Yoko Ono—in songs, on the backs of albums and in interviews. But Mick had almost nothing to say about Bianca, in his music or in the press, until the relationship began to sour a few years later, and there were plenty of gossip columnists who had nothing better to do than fill this factual vacuum with endless speculation. Someone noticed that

Mick and Bianca bore a remarkable resemblance to each other, and on this slender thread a heavy load of amateur psychoanalysis was hung.

Mick never offered much rejoinder to these idle speculations, and his relationship with Bianca remained an intensely private one; the Mick-and-Bianca-go-dancing candid photos and all the gossip column items were ciphers, revealing nothing. It seems likely that he kept the relationship private because he was genuinely in love, with a genuine flesh-and-blood woman, though their physical resemblance may well have been an additional turn-on.

During the months that followed Mick's wedding, Keith practically barricaded himself inside Nellcote, his villa in the south of France. He installed a studio in the basement and upgraded the equipment until it was good enough for the Stones to record their next album there. The drugs he needed to sustain his heroin addiction came to him, and so did musical friends like Gram Parsons, a former member of the Byrds, founder of the Flying Burrito Brothers and architect of country rock. Parsons also introduced Keith to several Southern musicians who later toured and recorded as Stones sidemen, and he taught Keith the songs, the sad inflections and other expressive fine points of country & western and particularly honky-tonk music.

Parsons stayed at Nellcote for months, playing informal duets with Keith almost every day. Eventually he returned to the U.S., where he recorded his masterpiece, *Grievous Angel*, before his drug-related death in 1973. Keith later made solo, not-for-release recordings of most of the country and honky-tonk evergreens Parsons taught him.

The Stones' tax exile was the first in a series of moves intended to give the band the complete control and financial mobility of the Swiss-bank upper crust. The next step came in April with the creation of their own label, Rolling Stones Records. The Stones chose At-

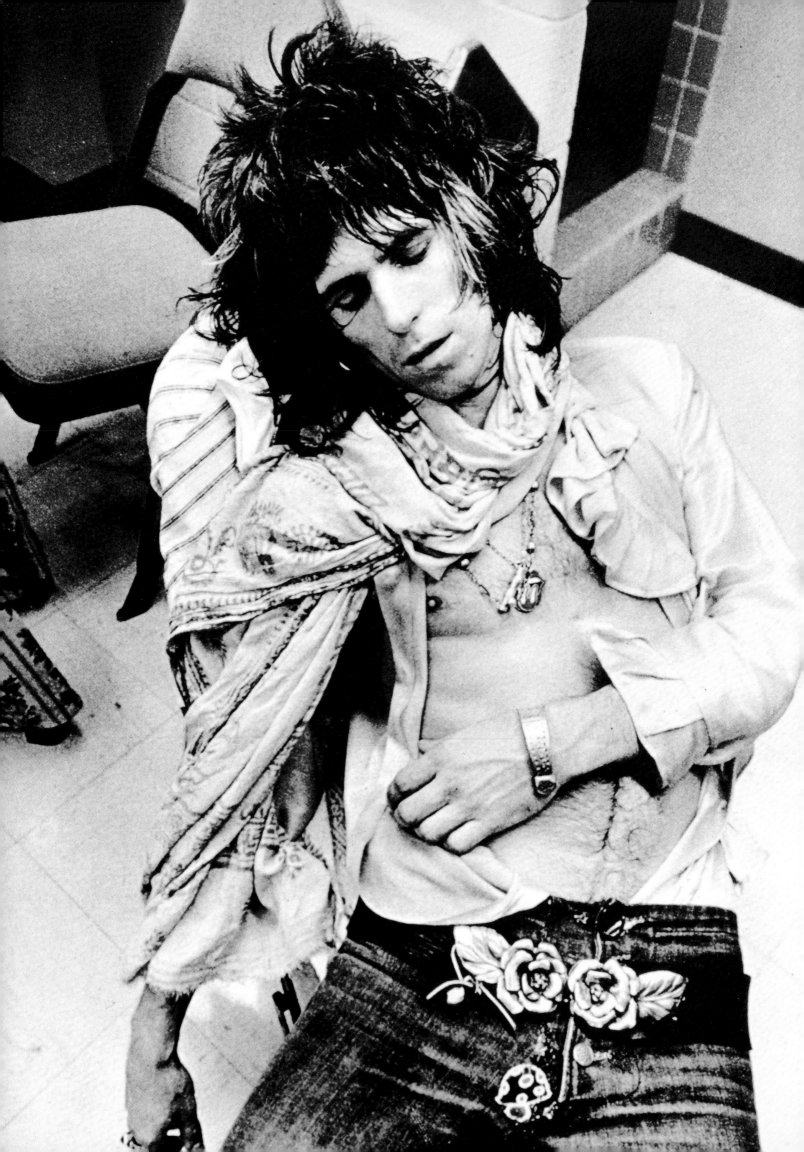

Well, you're drunk in the
     alley, baby,
With your clothes all torn
And your late night friends
Leave you in the cold gray
     dawn
Just seemed too many flies
     on you
I just can't brush them off.

Angels beating all their
     wings in time
With smiles on their faces
And a gleam right in their
     eyes.
Thought I heard one sigh for
     you
Come on up, come on up,
     now
Come on up, now.

May the good Lord shine a
     light on you,
Make every song you sing
     your favorite tune.
May the good Lord shine a
     light on you
Warm like the evening sun.

[SHINE A LIGHT]

lantic Records to distribute their releases and hired Marshall Chess, the
son of Chess Records founder Leonard
Chess and a hipster roughly their own
age, to serve as the company's president. Before the month was out, Rolling Stones had issued its first single,
"Brown Sugar."

Listeners had to work to make out
the words to "Brown Sugar," which
had been mixed down into the instrumental track and partly obscured, in
typical Stones fashion. Mick has recalled being profoundly influenced by
an interview with Fats Domino in
which the rotund hitmaker advised,
"You should never sing the words out
very clearly." Some of the lyrics on
"Satisfaction" and other Stones singles
were deliberately obscured, partly to
make the records more mysterious and
intriguing and partly to hide drug and
sex references from the censors. This
was the origin of the so-called Stones
mix—a vocalist fighting to be heard
over a wall of careening guitars and a
big bass and drum sound.

The first phrases most listeners
pulled out of the din of "Brown Sugar"
seemed like a welter of antifemale gibes
and dubious racial slurs. The song set a
pattern for controversy, the kind of
public do-they-or-don't-they that the
Stones loved to provoke—leading up to
the feminist controversy over the advertising campaign for *Black and Blue*
in 1976 and the Reverend Jesse Jack-
son's criticism of "Some Girls" in 1978.
As usual, though, the taunts in
"Brown Sugar" were a red herring.
The full lyric, three compact verses,
follows a slave ship's cargo from the
Gold Coast to a plantation in the English colonies. Mick notes with a certain
ironic relish that sexy black slave girls
always made "cold English blood" run
hot, and finally relates his own con-
quests of black women to the tradition
of slave mistresses and the exploitation
of blacks by his slave-trading ancestors.

THE song also has a sub-
text—the fascination with black culture and black expression that brought
the Stones together in the first place. In
those early days, black blues was almost a religion to them, and they pros-
elytized for their religion everywhere
they went—even in America, where

*Torn and frayed: Keith back-
stage in 1974.*

they insisted on sharing their first guest spot on the network television show "Shindig" with bluesman Howlin' Wolf. Such cheek was unheard of, but the incident wasn't isolated. The Stones hired black performers to open most of their subsequent tours—B. B. King, Ike and Tina Turner, Stevie Wonder. They had taken a great deal from black music and thought it was only fair to give something back. But by the early Seventies, the Stones' borrowings were being called ripoffs by critics and politicos. "Brown Sugar" answered the charge with tongue in cheek, pleading guilty to the exploitation of blacks with disarming candor and catching the band's most humorless detractors off guard.

"Brown Sugar" was the first single with the lapping tongue logo of Rolling Stones Records on the label; *Sticky Fingers* followed a week later. The bulging male crotch on the Andy Warhol cover and the lubricity of the title suggested that the accent would be on sex, and there is some supremely sexy rock & roll on *Sticky Fingers*—the seductive insistence of "Can't You Hear Me Knocking," the yearning intimacy of "Wild Horses," the juice and heat and drive of "Bitch" and "Brown Sugar." But the album is at least as concerned with drugs as it is with sex; Stones fans who habitually combed the band's LPs for drug references had a field day with it. "Brown Sugar" was a slang term for brown heroin, they noted, and the album ended with the hard-drug trilogy of "Sister Morphine," "Dead Flowers" (heroin again, as in crushed poppies) and "Moonlight Mile" ("with a head full of snow," cocaine). On *Sticky Fingers*, Mick and Keith seemed to be making a serious attempt to get something out of their drug experiences besides a rush.

But *Sticky Fingers* wasn't the triumph it might have been. Some of the arrangements lacked focus—there were too many guitars chugging away in the introduction to "Bitch," and the Santana-like instrumental tag to "Can't You Hear Me Knockin'" seemed gratuitous, tacked on. And too many of the songs attempted to provide hard-boiled accounts of lives lived on the edge but ended up sounding like druggy soap operas. ("Sister Morphine" was the worst offender, with its lurid Hollywood treatment of drug withdrawal.) All these defects were symptomatic of a more serious problem: a potentially debilitating self-consciousness was creeping into the Stones' music, and with it came a certain amount of overacting and cheap melodrama.

The Stones returned to Nellcote from July to November 1971 to record *Exile on Main Street*. It was more convenient for the band to come to Keith than for Keith to come to the band, for by this time the guitarist's drug addiction was the most pressing problem confronting the Rolling Stones. At least at Nellcote, privacy and the Stones security team made a bust less likely. And the band could work at its own pace, unhampered by studio schedules. The result was a double album that captured a confident rock & roll band at the height of its musical prowess. The rough, defiantly muddy sound emphasized the ensemble's guts and drive, burying Mick's vocals in the densest of all Stones mixes but capturing the Richards-Taylor twin-guitar assault at its most slashing and spirited, and the great Stones rhythm section sounding fiercely, urgently kinetic.

Some of the lyrics were disguised very efficiently indeed, perhaps because they were among the most personal the band had ever committed to vinyl. The Gram Parsons-influenced "Torn and Frayed," for example, commented on Keith's hard-drug problem with unsentimental clarity, successfully avoiding melodrama. In the "ballrooms and smelly bordellos/ And dressing rooms filled with parasites," Joe the guitar player (Keith transparently disguised) found himself getting more and more restless, and no wonder: "Joe's got a cough/ Sounds

Boating with Bianca and Princess Lee Radziwell: musically, the Stones might have been returning to basics, but Mick's lifestyle remained as glittery as ever.

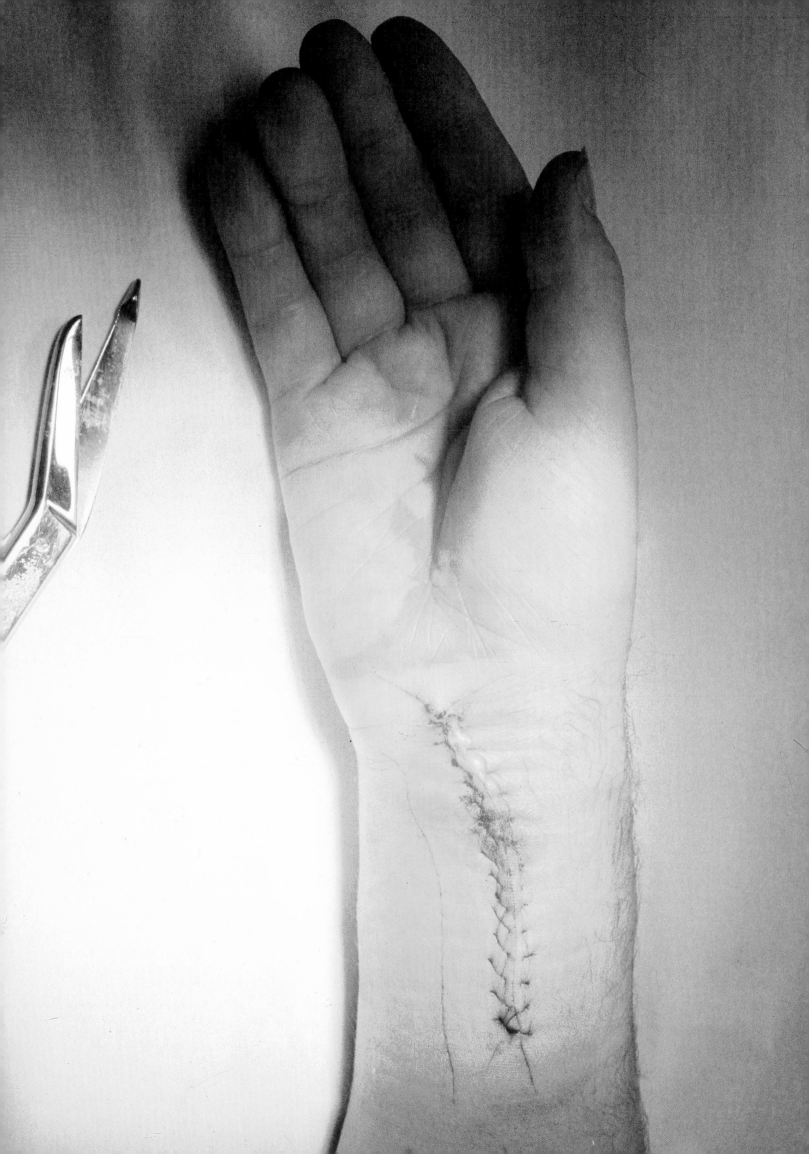

kinda rough/ Yeah, and the codeine to fix it/ Doctor prescribes/ Drugstore supplies/ Who's gonna help him to kick it?" The band was learning to live with Keith's problem, out of loyalty and because the music was still transcendent: "Just as long as the guitar plays/ Let it steal your heart away." Perhaps some of the other songs were addressed to the prodigal son as well. Hey you, soul survivor? You, turd on the run? C'mon, stop breaking down!

Exile on Main Street was released less than a month before the Stones kicked off their 1972 tour. Compared to *Let It Bleed* or *Beggar's Banquet*, or even *Sticky Fingers*, it sounded at first like a chaotic, sprawling mess. Stones albums often sounded impenetrable at first but always kicked in sooner or later. But critics, forced by newspaper and magazine deadlines to listen fast and take sides, registered disappointment and frustration at the music's blurred edges, the indecipherable lyrics, the apparent lack of contrast. Why was there filler like "Turd on the Run" and "Ventilator Blues" scattered among new classics like "Tumbling Dice," "Torn and Frayed" and "Happy"? *Exile*'s reputation soared only after the Stones followed it with the most abysmal records of their career.

When it was new, one could compare it only to the uneven but frequently captivating *Sticky Fingers* or to the near perfection of *Let It Bleed* and *Beggar's Banquet*. In this company, *Exile* comes up wanting.

Beggar's Banquet and *Let It Bleed* are classics of another sort; they are collections of superb rock & roll *songs*, and fine as the individual performances and the ensemble playing are, it's the songs and what they are saying that matter most in the end. *Exile*, on the other hand, is a great, defiant chunk of rock & roll *noise*. It defies the listener to delve into its murky depths, and it defies the Seventies' notion that rock & roll is above all an entertainment.

It's true that songs like "Tumbling Dice" and "Rip This Joint" are supremely entertaining, but even these songs have a careening momentum that sounds dangerous, a momentum that threatens to spin giddily out of control. And songs like "Shine a Light," "Torn and Frayed," the Robert Johnson blues "Stop Breaking Down" and "Soul Survivor" are entertaining only if you ignore their momentum and their message. Listen carefully, and they are intensely disturbing vignettes, warnings that decay and death are waiting in the wings and may even be

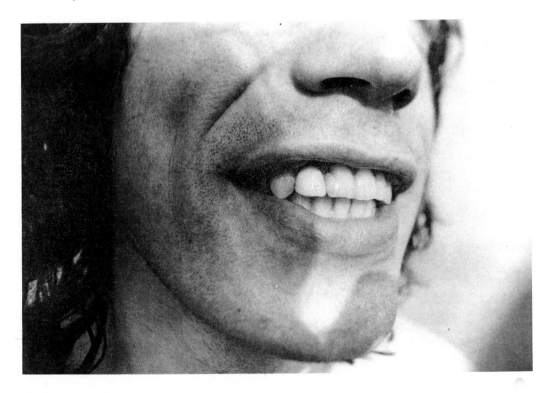

The year was already 1975, and still the press persevered: Mick rips open his right wrist—click. Has diamond set into his front tooth—click, click. Overleaf: Just as the Stones had never really tried to replace Brian Jones in their lineup, neither did they seek out another blues soloist to take the place of the departed Mick Taylor. Former Face Ron Wood (whose brother Art had been the original singer in Alexis Korner's Blues Incorporated) joined in on the Stones' 1975 U.S. tour—adding more raucous spirit than serious musicianship—and by the time they released Black and Blue the following April, he was a full-fledged member of the group.

calling the tune. Several lyric excerpts are reprinted amid Robert Frank's photo images of a Main Street America that died more than a decade ago. "I don't want to talk about Jesus," says one, "I just wanna see his face." The other: "I gave you the diamonds, you give me disease." Barbed, deadly lines like these poke out of the thick, swirling sound mix at every turn, and the music just roars along toward some unimaginable apocalypse—until the final track, "Soul Survivor," which announces that *this* rock & roll band is determined to survive, whatever the cost.

In retrospect, *Exile* seems a startling show of strength and solidarity from a collection of rich, jaded stars that was no longer a band in any real sense. Mick and Keith, who took on more of the producer's role during the sessions, worked well together in the studio, and Charlie, Bill and Mick Taylor performed their roles efficiently and often brilliantly. The shows on the 1972 tour were consistently exhilarating. But when they weren't working, the Stones went their separate ways. In December, after the tour ended, Mick and Bianca and Keith and Anita took sudden trips overseas, for reasons as wildly disparate as their lifestyles.

Mick and Bianca flew to Managua with 2,000 typhoid inoculations for earthquake victims in Bianca's native Nicaragua. Meanwhile, Keith and Anita departed abruptly from southern France after reports of their heroin use led to warrants being issued for their arrest.

Exile may seem flawed compared to the albums that preceded it, but it sounds positively concise compared to the ones that followed. As Keith grew increasingly preoccupied with and sapped by his drug habit, and as Mick coped with his social responsibilities and celebrity, the Stones' music seemed to unravel. Their next three albums— *Goat's Head Soup* (1973), *It's Only Rock 'N Roll* (1974) and *Black and Blue* (1976)—are actually a single, rambling work. They draw on the same pool of material, and none of them deals with a particular time period or theme or has a really distinct point of view. Even worse, the arrangements and mixes lack the precision, focus and punch of the Stones' finer work. And no wonder! It was difficult to corral all the Stones in the same studio at the same time during the mid-Seventies, and even more difficult to psych them into making music together like a real band. So Mick and Keith would try

Keith and class wheels in Montauk. Right: Charlie chatting on the beach.

this song and that, record batches of material, finish what they could, add overdubs or guest soloists and then sift through what they had and choose the eight or ten finished songs that seemed to work best together. And that would be the next LP.

Even when they came up with decent songs (and throwaways like "Dancing with Mr. D," "Luxury" and "Crazy Mama" are barely that), the mid-Seventies Stones tended to clutter them with slapdash arrangements. Their best rock & roll had always been built around Keith's solid guitar riffs; additional parts were added sparingly, to make the rhythm pull as well as push, to emphasize a particular color or mood. Mixing was the final step, intended to focus the already concise arrangements and give the finished tracks a diamondlike hardness and sparkle. Too many mid-Seventies Stones tracks, rockers and ballads alike, sounded like they'd been arranged at the mixing session by pulling out bits and pieces of guitar and keyboard parts that had been arbitrarily piled up in the first place, without any conception of the finished product.

Some listeners concluded that the band was tired of trying to equal its earlier achievements and had decided to deliberately trash its own reputation. The bitter truth was that *Goat's Head Soup*, *It's Only Rock 'N Roll* and *Black and Blue* were what the Rolling Stones sounded like with Keith preoccupied and the others bored and dispirited. It didn't make much difference when Mick and Keith took over full production, using their Glimmer Twins pseudonym, after *Goat's Head Soup*. It didn't even make much difference when Mick Taylor, bored to tears after the sessions that produced most of *It's Only Rock 'N Roll*, left the band in late 1974, on the eve of the *Black and Blue* sessions, forcing them to record as a quartet again—with guest guitarists providing most of the hot solos. It didn't matter, because the Stones had lost that delicate balance of Apollonian economy and symmetry and Dionysian passion and thrust. And they had lost their nerve.

Despite that, the mid-Seventies albums weren't total washouts. They included a few tender, memorably lyrical ballads—"Winter," "Memory Motel," "Fool to Cry." Mick was trying to expand the emotional range of his vocals and to firm up the sound of his voice, when he wasn't walking through hideous self-parodies like "Dancing with Mr. D," "Dance Little Sister" and "Hot Stuff." But when he sang "It's sometimes wise not to grow up," and

Fashion doyenne Diana Vreeland bestockinged backstage during the glitzy 1975 tour. Below: Bianca—no, Mick!—going under the makeup brush.

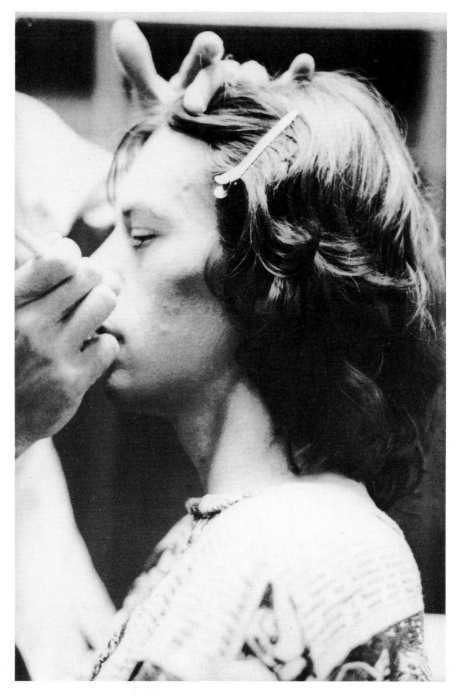

added "Don't you think it's just about time to hide away" as an afterthought in the rambling, disorganized "100 Years Ago," there wasn't much to do but agree and put on *Between the Buttons* instead.

Some Stones fans who'd followed the band for years simply wrote them off. Some got mad but kept hoping. Some even gave them the benefit of the doubt. For, while the Stones had surely bottomed out, by this time so had many of the other surviving superstars of Sixties rock. The Beatles dream had bitten the dust long ago; the Stones choogling through "Silver Train" still rocked with more conviction than Paul McCartney's "Silly Love Songs." John Lennon was silent. Bob Dylan was making albums like *Desire* and *Street-Legal*, pale efforts compared to his masterpieces of the middle and late Sixties. And the most popular of the younger groups and soloists were simply *recycling* the Sixties with an added layer of up-to-date studio sheen that fooled a surprisingly large number of fans, kids and otherwise, into thinking they were hearing something new. There wasn't much rock & roll around that was really worthy of the name—not until 1976 or so. Then, in a few sleazy, sweaty little clubs in New York and London,

something happened. Suddenly kids in their teens and early twenties were making their own rock & roll, and if it was rough and crude and boisterously abrasive, it could also be deliriously exciting. Almost overnight, it seemed, the music press was full of interviews with performers who called themselves Johnny Rotten and Cheetah Chrome and Poly Styrene and called the Stones and the other Sixties holdouts rich, boring old farts. The new arrivals, the punk rockers, thought just enough of the Who to throw one of their own lyrics back at them, and at their contemporaries: "Why don't you all just f-f-fade away?" Joe Strummer of the Clash (by 1983 attempting to rationalize their *own* rock-star lifestyles) made up a singalong for punk audiences that went "no more Beatles, Stones or Who in 1977." It was a kiss-off and a challenge.

THE advent of punk rock offered the Stones and their few remaining musical contemporaries only

The Stones' 1975 tour defined the arena-rock genre, featuring a mammoth sound enhanced by keyboardist Billy Preston (left) and percussionist Ollie Brown, and a phallic "finger" designed to keep the kids interested—and their parents steaming. One tabloid moralist castigated the Stones for flaunting "the timeless values that have made us a great people. Things that have a lot to do with God, a flag and a country. Corny? Well, maybe...."

two real options: rejuvenation or the scrapheap. But the rejuvenation of the Rolling Stones had already begun, and was proceeding at its own deliberate pace. Mick Taylor had unwittingly moved the Stones toward recovery by quitting. Taylor was the most accomplished technician who ever served as a Stone; at their best, the Richards-Taylor Rolling Stones were sleeker and more streamlined than any other edition of the band. Yet some hard-core Brian Jones loyalists snorted that Taylor never really fit in. A blues guitarist with a jazzman's flair for melodic invention, Taylor was never a rock & roller and never a showman. The day after he quit, Keith sent him a telegram whose very brevity tells the story of Stones II: "Really enjoyed playing with you for the last five years. Thanks for all the turn-ons. Best wishes and love."

The Stones tried out several guitarists for Mick Taylor's spot as principal soloist and lead man while recording *Black and Blue*, but when they hit the road for their 1975 American tour, the guitarist standing alongside Keith was his friend Ron Wood. Woody was younger than the other Stones, but he had known them since the early Sixties, when he was a precocious kid tagging along to his older brothers' gigs with Alexis Korner and Cyril Davis. Woody first heard the Stones at the Crawdaddy Club and the Marquee. In 1975, he was still a member of Rod Stewart's sloppy but spirited Faces, a Stones favorite, but he'd been playing with Keith, informally and on his own solo sessions, for several years. Stewart was enjoying a successful solo career and thinking about leaving the Faces when Wood took a leave of absence to tour with the Stones. And when Mick and Keith offered the cocky guitarist a permanent gig, Stewart saw his moment—the Faces were finished anyway. So Rod and Ronnie, who'd been best buddies, writing songs and making music and boozing and screwing and brawling together for years, went on one last whopping bender and told the Faces they were both leaving. Stewart started his own band, and Woody became a Stone.

The Stones hadn't tried to replace Brian Jones with another bright, mercurial multiinstrumentalist, and they didn't try to replace Mick Taylor with another virtuoso. Woody was an inconsistent and often a distressingly ragged player; he was anything but slick.

Preceding page: The Rolling Stones—with Billy Preston (second from left) and Ollie Brown—after their Los Angeles concert in July 1975. "Nobody really understands about the effect that certain rhythms have on people," Keith said, "but our bodies beat. We're only alive because the heartbeat keeps going all the time. And also, certain sounds can kill." Right: raking it in. Overleaf: Mick in Barbados, soaking up sounds. Black music was the linchpin of the Stones' career, and they've remained avid fans. Jagger has appeared on "Saturday Night Live" singing with Jamaican star Peter Tosh, and reggae and other island rhythms have played an increasingly important part in the Stones' latter-day music.

If I could stick a knife in my
   heart
Suicide right on the stage,
Would it be enough for your
   teenage lust?
Would it help ease the pain?
Ease your brain.

If I could dig deep down in
   my heart
Feelings would flood on the
   page
Would it satisfy ya?
Would it slide on by ya?
Would you think the boy's
   insane?
He's insa-ya-yane.

I said I know it's only rock
   'n' roll but I like it,
Well I like it, I like it, I like
   it—
I said can't you see this old
   boy's getting lonely.

[IT'S ONLY ROCK 'N' ROLL]

But like Keith, he was versatile, equally adept at simple, biting leads and
slash-and-burn rhythm. And instead of
assigning him lead or rhythm chores on
each tune, Keith worked with him the
way he'd worked with Brian, practicing and experimenting, adding and dis-
carding, figuring out two-guitar parts
that would complement each other by
a time-consuming process of trial and
error. Ronnie began to make an important contribution to the Stones as soon
as he joined the 1975 tour. He brought
energy and high spirits, a perpetual
cockeyed grin, jokes and pranks—in
short, a boyish, Faces-style sense of
fun, something that had been in short
supply among the Stones for some time.

Onstage, nobody was safe from the
rampaging Wood. Keith had to keep
his eyes open to shape Ronnie's playing
and cue him into chording or soloing,
embellishing or laying back. Mick,
who'd had unchallenged run of the
stage since the mid-Sixties, would suddenly find Woody outflanking him
with a mad charge at the audience or
sneaking up behind him and mugging.
Bill Wyman couldn't even stand safely
in his sacrosanct "Ol' Stoneface" corner without Woody baiting him like a
tourist teasing a Beefeater. And Charlie found he had more leeway to make
up new rhythm patterns with Ronnie
and Keith bouncing syncopated cross
rhythms off him from opposite ends of
the stage. The Stones were having a
good time onstage again, and before
Woody had been with them a year,
they were already planning to record a
live album. It wasn't going to be an
ordinary live album—a condensed
arena show—either. The band decided
to vary its concert schedule by working in some dates in small theaters and
nightclubs, with a recording stop at the
El Mocambo in Toronto.

BY February 1977, the
Stones seemed to be on an upswing—
except for Keith, who was so loaded
that he mistook the people who went
through Anita's twenty-eight pieces of
luggage at the Toronto airport for
Stones hirelings. In fact, the helpful
folks were Mounties, and when they
found ten grams of hash and a black-
ened spoon, they arrested Anita and
began plotting an even bigger catch.
Three days later, a small army of
Mounties stormed into the rooms
Keith and Anita had rented at the Harbour Castle Hotel and busted Keith for
possession of one ounce of high-quality
heroin, a large enough quantity for a

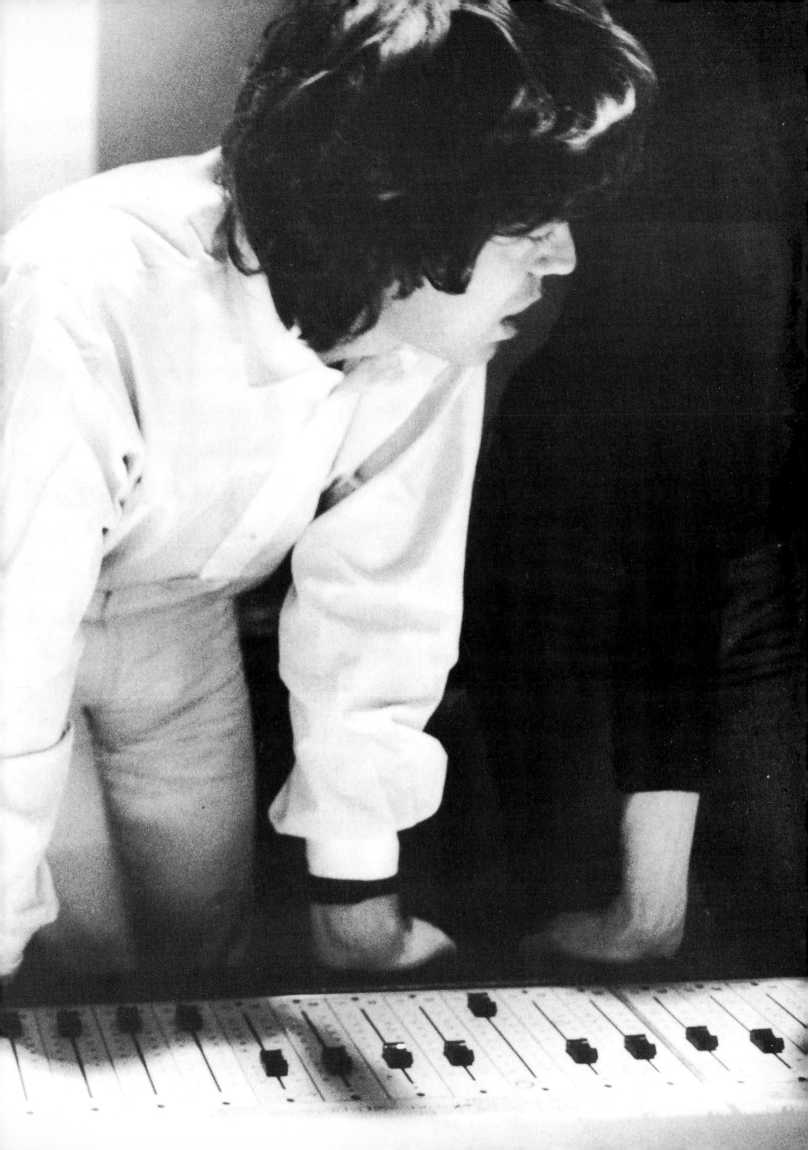

Preceding page: Mick and Keith in the studio in Paris, 1978. Their songs take shape over the course of years, with Jagger and Richards tinkering with each track until it seems ready for inclusion on an album. Right: Bill in Antibes in 1977. The bassist finally got a life of his own going in France, collaborating on a book of photographs with artist Marc Chagall, composing the soundtrack for a Ryan O'Neal movie, Green Ice, and even scoring a hit single with the whimsical "Je Suis Un Rockstar."

trafficking charge and a possible sentence of seven years to life.

Headline writers had been asking if "this could be the last time" since the Stones tour of 1969, but this time it looked like the answer might be yes. Keith's arrest record included a recent coke bust in England, a fine in France in 1972 for being caught with hash, cocaine and heroin, and various other drug offenses going back almost a decade. Nobody seemed to be able to recall the last time someone had beaten a trafficking charge in Canada. The Stones went on with their shows at the El Mocambo and recorded some gritty blues and reggae that turned out to be the only decent music on their third and sloppiest live album, 1977's *Love You Live* (the rest of the cuts were recorded before Woody had been effectively integrated into the band). And then the Canadian visit turned into a media circus.

Margaret Trudeau, Canada's first lady, attended a show at the El Mocambo, returned to the Harbour Castle with the band and was spotted several days later in one of the hotel's hallways, dressed in a bathrobe and still partying. At least she distracted the self-appointed guardians of morality writing for Canada's daily newspapers. They waxed indignant when she followed the Stones to New York and temporarily forgot about Keith,

who had to stay in Toronto until he was formally charged and given a trial date. Stones publicist Paul Wasserman arrived in New York looking haggard. "Why do you look so beat?" a friend who hadn't been following the events in Toronto inquired. "Because we've never toppled a friendly foreign government before," he wryly replied.

The Stones' legal team managed to secure permission for Keith to leave Canada to work, and the Stones' 1978 summer tour of the U.S. and the release of *Some Girls* that June went ahead on schedule. Keith, exuding optimism when talk turned to his upcoming trial in October, at least managed to get a song for *Some Girls* out of the predicament. "Watch my tail lights fading/ There ain't a dry eye in the house," he moaned like a cross between an Appalachian hillbilly and an alley cat. "I'm gonna find my way to heaven 'cause I did my time in hell/ I wasn't looking too good, but I was feeling real well." But the repeated refrain was more sobering: "After all is said and done/ I did all right and had my fun/ But I will walk before they make me run."

Mick contributed some humor of his own to the album. "Now we're respected in society," he boasted in a raucous, utterly traditional Chuck Berry-style rocker, "Respectable." He used the tune to sling some darts at Bianca; the couple was headed for divorce. And he couldn't resist adding a scene that was amusing, if somewhat unlikely: "We're talking heroin with the President/ Yes, it's a problem, sir, but it can be bent."

The rest of *Some Girls* ranged from Mick's embarrassing redneck imitation in "Far Away Eyes" to the fresh, punky riff tune "Shattered," to the soaring Motown cover "Imagination." "Miss You," released at the height of the "Disco Sucks" hysteria, can be seen, now that the schism has given way to the punk-funk era, as the band's most impressive single in years. Mick sounded determined to overcome his

The Stones' career faced its most severe crunch in Canada in February 1977. First, Anita Pallenberg was arrested at Toronto Airport. Then, three days later, Mounties busted Keith in the Harbour Castle Hotel and confiscated one ounce of high-quality heroin—under Canadian law, an amount large enough to justify a drug-trafficking charge. In a song that later appeared on the Stones' Some Girls album, Keith promised, "I will walk before they make me run." In the end, that proved unnecessary: when the guitarist returned to Toronto to plead guilty to the drug charge, he looked unusually fit, and the judge surprised virtually everyone by letting him off with a warning, a year's suspended sentence and the stipulation that he return to Toronto to perform a concert for charity.

This low down bitchin' got
  my poor feet a-itchin'
You know, you know the
  deuce is still wild.
Baby, I can't stay
You got to roll me and call
  me the tumblin' dice.

Always in a hurry
I never stop to worry
Don't you see the time
  flashin' by,
Honey, got no money
I'm all sixes and sevens and
  nines.

Say now, baby, I'm the rank
  outsider
You can be my partner in
  crime,
But, baby, I can't stay
You got to roll me and call
  me the tumblin'
Roll me and call me the
  tumblin' dice.

[TUMBLING DICE]

decadent playboy image and flex his musical muscles to make the Stones *mean* something again. This time, his vocal wasn't buried behind the Stones' brand of rock & roll murk. It was right out front, and it was wounded, haunting, entirely believable. Mick was admitting, for the first time since his marriage to Bianca, that he was as vulnerable, as capable of being hurt by a lover's absence or indifference, as anyone else. The admission somehow made him sound genuinely, unaffectedly sexy. "Miss You" was a performance, a brilliant one, but it was personal, open, utterly unlike the calculated playacting in which Mick had

indulged on so many mid-Seventies Stones recordings. The rest of *Some Girls* was an improvement, too. It wasn't a great album, but it was so much better than its predecessors that plenty of people gladly mistook it for one.

When Keith returned to Toronto to plead guilty, the judge surprised virtually everyone by letting him off with a warning, a year's suspended sentence, and the stipulation that he should return to Toronto one more time to perform for the benefit of charity. If Keith had walked into the courtroom with pinned pupils, unable to prove he was off drugs, things might well have turned out differently. But he had kicked heroin, and knowing that another heroin bust could mean the end of his career as a Rolling Stone —and even his freedom—he stayed clean. In the months that followed, he underwent a startling transformation. It was already evident in April 1979, when he sang and played with Ron Wood's New Barbarians at two concerts benefitting the Canadian National Institute for the Blind.

The dates were the first in a month-long Barbarians tour, nominally a lavish promotion for Woody's latest solo album, *Gimme Some Neck*. But Woody was more than willing to share the stage with Keith and to use musicians Keith had been wanting to play with for a long time: drummer Ziggy Modeliste from the Meters, jazz superbassist Stanley Clarke (whose showy, sixteenth-note style Keith methodically pruned), longtime Stones sidekick Bobby Keys on sax and Woody's Faces buddy Ian McLagan on keyboards. The surprise of the tour was Keith's soul, blues and honky-tonk singing, which was controlled and heartfelt and started rumors that a Keith Richards solo album was imminent.

But it's highly unlikely that Keith will ever make a solo album while the Rolling Stones last, because the Stones are *his* band. When he feels the need to

make music outside the group, he collects the players of his choice, rents a studio and records, but strictly for his own edification and amusement. His pockets are always bulging with cassettes, some collecting singles of Fifties doo-wop or the Everly Brothers or reggae or down-home blues, some the latest mixes from his private sessions. He's recorded a mean blues-shuffle version of "Key to the Highway" as a one-man band—vocals, two guitar parts and piano. He's taped sessions with Buddy Holly's original Crickets, the crack reggae rhythm team of Sly Dunbar and Robbie Shakespeare and top Nashville sessionmen—and there are videos as well.

One video preserves a night at the Checkerboard Lounge on Chicago's black South Side, where Keith, Ronnie, Mick and Ian Stewart sat in with Muddy Waters and his band after playing a stadium date on the Stones' 1981 tour. It's a remarkable tape, not only for Muddy's evident delight that his children have come to call and for the bluesy immediacy and admirably self-effacing economy of Keith and Ronnie's guitar interplay, but for Mick, too. Singing, alternating verses with the toughest of living blues singers for a suspicious and demanding black blues crowd, shaking his ass, ad-libbing innuendoes and summoning more than enough power to get a stadium crowd on its feet, Mick is the surprise hit of the set. Even Muddy drops his inscrutable mask and looks startled before he digs in and gives Mick a run for his money.

Some Girls (1978) was the first album that announced the Stones' resurgence; *Emotional Rescue* (1980) consolidated its gains. On *Rescue*, the entire band sounds freshly energized and unwilling to craft arrangements and cut tracks according to proven Stones formulas. The song "Emotional Rescue" has a cocky, utterly original rhythmic lilt that's part reggae, part funk, part straight-ahead rock & roll. Charlie Watts called the rhythm "half-reggae," but whatever one calls it, "Emotional Rescue" and several other songs on the album offer unexpectedly fresh and vital rhythmic directions. And *Emotional Rescue* expanded on the more open emotional stance of "Miss You," with Keith getting into the act in a revealing, typically outspoken love-hate song chronicling the end of his years-long love affair with Anita Pallenberg, "All about You."

Some Girls and *Emotional Rescue* were good, frequently inspiring, but

As Mick's marriage to Bianca began falling apart, he took up with Jerry Hall, a Texas-bred fashion model and the former girlfriend of Roxy Music leader Bryan Ferry. Right: Mick's short-lived elder-statesman look.

1981's *Tattoo You* was the real break-through. Some of the songs on that album were as old as the *Goat's Head Soup* sessions, but this time, they fit into an overall plan. *Tattoo You* has a perspective, a point of view—and the warmth of "Miss You," this time suffusing the entire album. And it has a radically new Stones sound to match—clean, crisp, powerfully percussive, with Charlie Watts' incisively kinetic drumming, still the best in rock and getting better, mixed way out front. The sound comes courtesy of Bob Clearmountain, who mixed the subsequent *Still Life* album and the film of the 1981 tour, *Let's Spend the Night Together*. But Clearmountain didn't *create* the sound. He heard the clarity and punch that were already there and brought them to the fore.

On *Tattoo You*, the Rolling Stones sound like a great rock & roll *band* again, but they aren't the old Stones magically revitalized, they're something new. If much of their Seventies work seems futile or depressing in retrospect, the futility and the depression were probably inevitable. The Stones were growing older and learning to cope with it, as were their fans. If they were no longer snotty young outsiders looking to get inside and intending to

trash the premises upon admittance, who were they exactly? It has taken them much of the past decade to find out, but the Stones of the Eighties seem to have a handle on who they are, and a clear understanding of who they aren't. They aren't kids or rebel anarchists or demons anymore. But they're still supremely self-confident, even a little arrogant; they're still a rock & roll band.

Only they're a *grown-up* rock & roll band, with fans ranging in age from under ten to sixty or more, and with a history as rich and various as the histories of the early bluesmen and first-generation rockers they've always admired. They have something else in common with those blues singers and early rockers, too; they have their dignity. When the Stones get onstage now, they don't try to pass themselves off as adolescents. They're professionals doing what they do best—playing blistering rock & roll.

It's fashionable these days for rock fans and critics who grew up listening to the Stones and are now pushing forty themselves to laugh at Mick and Keith and the rest of them, to call them old and creaky and suggest they retire to their rocking chairs. Mick hasn't entirely outgrown his vanity, and he

"With Ronnie," Keith has said, "we seem to be able to get back to the original idea of the Stones, when Brian was with us in 1962, '63." This page: the family man at home.

hasn't learned to ignore these gibes, despite the fact that he's in better physical shape and more in control of his singing than he was ten years ago. But he doesn't mope anymore when journalists ask him when he's going to retire. He gets combative and points out that the Stones never addressed their music specifically to young people, and that bluesmen like Howlin' Wolf were in their forties when they started recording, in their sixties when they finally stopped turning somersaults and doing back flips onstage, and still performing when they died. Mick was singing songs by seventy-year-old bluesmen when he was twenty, and he never sang about being a kid at the high-school hop. And when he'd get onstage with someone like Muddy Waters, who in his late sixties could still rock a joint to the rafters, Mick Jagger kicks ass. Even Keith looks remarkably healthy. He trained for the Stones' 1981 tour by jogging every day through the Massachusetts countryside, and on that tour, he made the most riveting music of his career.

The 1981 tour was bigger than anything the Beatles could have envisioned and handily eclipsed its closest competition, the Who's farewell tour the following year. It made more money than any tour in rock & roll history, but the statistics only blinded those who were deaf to the music. Some

Charlie has been called the greatest drummer in the history of rock & roll. With wife Shirley, below.

Keith—now separated from his longtime common-law wife Anita, by whom he has two children—says he's found real love again with Patti Hansen, whose separate and very successful career as a photo model suits Keith's own nonclinging ways.

shows were better than others, as they always are with the Stones. For the Stones are now virtually the only band playing to stadium crowds that isn't afraid to make mistakes.

But a band that's too slick to make mistakes isn't playing rock & roll, it's play-acting. And when today's Stones are clicking, as they were when they played the 1981 tour's most intimate date, at the Fox Theater in Atlanta, they are unforgettable.

Backstage before the Atlanta show, Keith and Charlie and Ian McLagan passed a bottle and sang caterwauling barbershop harmony. Just after the Stray Cats opened the show, Ronnie came trudging into the theater's rear entrance, a flight bag in each hand, his eyes on the ground and his head somewhere in the clouds. Before he looked up and realized where he was, he had walked right out onto the stage, into the spotlight. The Stray Cats glanced over at him, puzzled. Was he embarrassed? Not at all. He retraced his steps, stopped by Mick's dressing room to tell him what had happened and have a laugh about it, and then went to join the excruciatingly out-of-tune singing in the adjoining room. Mick grinned and shook his head. "If this band was ever going to get really slick," he mused, "it would've happened a long time ago."

When they were good and ready, the Stones hit the stage. The sound was clear, and so beautifully balanced that even a casual listener could distinguish Keith's guitar from Ronnie's, and Ian Stewart's hammered boogie-woogie from Ian McLagan's Jerry Lee Lewis rock & roll. Mick was singing hard and true, but it was Keith who pushed the band into playing its best and then playing better. Nobody was sitting down, and the momentum kept building, song after song, until the Stones were rocking harder than Little Richard or Chuck Berry, as hard as anyone ever rocked.

Charlie, not used to playing so aggressively, kept trying to bring the ferocious energy level down a hair, but Keith would turn on him, jump onto the drum riser and pump his guitar wildly up and down until Charlie broke into one of his megawatt grins and gave in. Wyman was reeling off brawny lines that heaved at the rhythm from underneath, and he flashed Keith one of his rare smiles. When the curtain went down, it was Keith who accepted the bouquet of roses, who took the final bow. He'd been the spark plug of the tour's hottest show—and the Stones had rocked and rolled and raged like a hurricane.

And isn't that exactly what rock & roll is supposed to do? If a good backbeat can make the gray men who legislate morality shiver in their boots, a good backbeat can strengthen and inspire and liberate and heal the rest of us. The age of the musicians and the size of their personal fortunes should be, and is, irrelevant. In West Africa, the drummers who preserve the rhythms of the gods and call them down to possess and cleanse the faithful often receive lavish gifts from wealthy patrons and can amass fortunes equal to a king's. And Africans who know music say a drummer can't play the sacred rhythm with real authority and spiritual force until he's at least forty. The Rolling Stones may be just hitting their stride.

As Charlie has remained in England, so Bill (below with his wife, Astrid) has stayed put in the south of France.

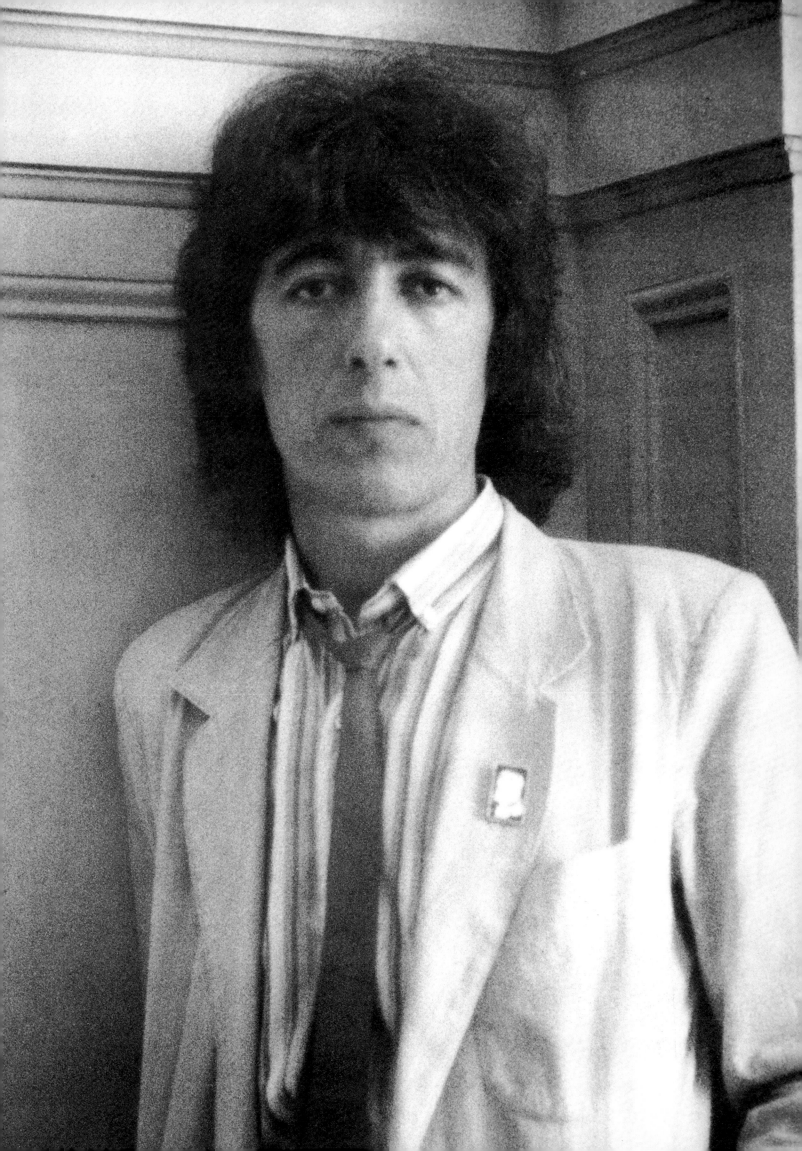

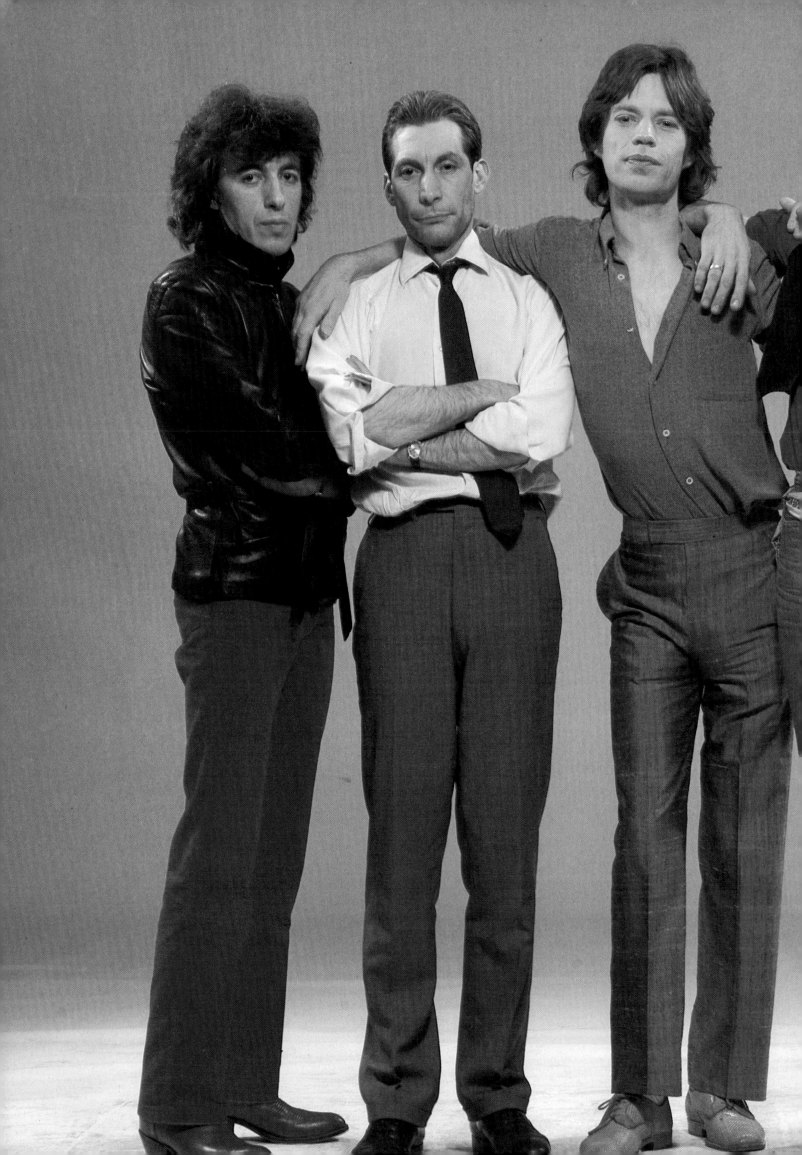

After more than two decades, the Stones made it into the Eighties with their critical reputation once again intact. Older now, and visibly battered by the years, they nevertheless offered proof that rock & roll can still be compelling long after youth itself—and its attendant illusions—have flown.

Addenda

Robert Palmer's Rolling Stones Top Ten: A Selected Discography

The Rolling Stones (England's Newest Hit-makers), 1964. Off and running, strutting their stuff, the Stones more than make up for one or two miscalculations by transforming Chicago blues and Memphis soul into their own brand of rock & roll.

Out of Our Heads, 1965. By mid-1965, the Stones have put their awkward moments behind them. This album, released with somewhat different contents in England and the U.S., is the definitive portrait of the Stones as a resourceful and inventive cover band, either way; the U.S. album has more hits.

Big Hits (High Tide and Green Grass), 1966. The British edition of this essential singles compilation is more complete, with "Have You Seen Your Mother Baby, Standing in the Shadow?," "Little Red Rooster," and the band's very first single, "Come On," added to the more familiar American A sides; avoid the much skimpier U.S. release.

Aftermath, 1966. Most of the tunes are still blues-based, but with the band pulling off one inspired, unexpected arranging triumph after another, and Brian Jones adding everything from mallet instruments to dulcimer and sitar, who'd notice? This is the first Stones album made up entirely of Jagger–Richards originals, and again the English version, with fourteen songs, is superior.

Between the Buttons, 1967. A grab-bag, not a unified piece of work like *Aftermath*, but track for track, this is prime Stones. Keith's maturing power-chord concepts, Mick's expanding list of lyrical obsessions and vocal nuances, and Brian's addition of various wind instruments to his arsenal contrast bracingly with the rhythm section's joyous, supple drive.

Beggar's Banquet, 1968. Jimmy Miller, the Stones' first real producer, turns a sheaf of great songs into a great album, with a new acoustic delicacy added to the band's customary drive, some ingenious self-referential image-making, and Brian Jones's otherworldly slide guitar stylings, one of the most glorious and mournful sounds in all of rock.

Let It Bleed, 1969. Here's the heart of the Stones' dark, uncompromising existential vision—you can't always get what you want, and murder's just a shot away. Here's Keith Richards at an awesome creative peak, stacking pealing, viscerally compelling guitar riffs like so much kindling wood. And here are the Midnight Rambler, the Monkey Man, the haunted bluesman, and the honky-tonk tarts, all dressed up for your very own nightmare.

Exile on Main Street, 1972. Recorded mostly in the basement of Keith's French villa, this is primarily a hot, raw, messy, utterly authentic, and more than generous helping of careening, almost-out-of-control rock & roll noise, and only secondarily a collection of songs that speak to the human condition, and the Stones' more problematic one, with rare candor and insight.

Some Girls, 1978. The Stones are taking chances again, after a near-fatal mid-Seventies slump, and if they fall on their faces at least once ("Far Away Eyes"), the rest of the time they soar. Taillights fading, not a dry eye in the house, but this is really more like starting over.

Tattoo You, 1981. Humanity, humility, Mick's magnificently detailed and yearning vocals, indelible sax solos by none other than Sonny Rollins, craft, maturity—this is rock & roll, and I like it, yes, I do.

Selected Bibliography

Aftel, Mandy. *Death of a Rolling Stone: The Brian Jones Story*. New York: Delilah Books, 1982.

Dalton, David. *The Rolling Stones: The First Twenty Years*. New York: Alfred A. Knopf, 1981.

Editors of Rolling Stone. *The Rolling Stone Interviews*. New York: St. Martin's Press/Rolling Stone Press, 1981.

Greenfield, Robert. *S.T.P.: A Journey through America with the Rolling Stones*. New York: Saturday Review Press/E.P. Dutton, 1974.

Hardy, Phil and Laing, Dave, eds. *The Encyclopedia of Rock*. St. Albans, U.K.: Panther, 1976.

Logan, Nick and Woffinden, Bob, eds. *The Illustrated Encyclopedia of Rock*. New York: Harmony, 1977, 1982.

Miller, Jim, ed. *The Rolling Stone Illustrated History of Rock & Roll*. New York: Random House/Rolling Stone Press, 1976, 1980.

Miller, John. *African Rhythms and African Sensibility*. Chicago: The University of Chicago Press, 1980.

Sanchez, Tony. *Up and Down with the Rolling Stones*. New York: William Morrow and Company, 1979.

Schaffner, Nicholas. *The British Invasion: From the First Wave to the New Wave*. New York: McGraw-Hill, 1982.

Thompson, Robert F. *African Art in Motion*. Berkeley: University of California Press, 1974.

The Rolling Stones Complete. London: Omnibus Press/EMI Music Publishing Ltd., 1981.

Credits

(Page 1) Dezo Hoffman, Rex Features/RDR Productions; (11, 12, 13) Syndication International/Photo Trends; (17) Collection, Tom Beach; (20-21) Dezo Hoffman, Rex Features/RDR Productions; (22-23) David Bailey/Camera Press; (24) Rex Features/RDR Productions; (25) ABC-TV; (26-27) Collection, Tom Beach; (28-29) Pictorial Press; (29) London Express/Pictorial Parade; (30-31) Rex Features/RDR Productions; (32-33) London Features International; (34-35) Syndication International/Photo Trends; (36, 36-37) London Express/Pictorial Parade; (39) Photo World/FPG; (40-41) S. Norris/Photo Trends; (42-43) F. Bauman/Photo Trends; (45, 48) Syndication International/Photo Trends; (49) The Michael Ochs Archives; (50-51) Syndication International/Photo Trends; (52) Pictorial Press; (53) Norman Parkinson/Photo Trends; (54, 55) Gered Mankowitz; (56-57) Jim Marshall; (58, 59, 60, 61, 63, 64, 65, 66, 69) Gered Mankowitz; (70-71) Jim Marshall; (72-73, 75, 76, 77, 78-79, 80) Gered Mankowitz; (81, 83) Syndication International/Photo Trends; (84-85, 86) Collection, Tom Beach; (87) Michael Cooper; (88) United Press International; (90, 91, 92, 93, 95) Michael Cooper; (97) Syndication International/Photo Trends; (98-99, 100-101, 102-103, 104, 105, 107, 108-109, 110-111, 112-113, 114) Michael Cooper; (116-117) Syndication International/Photo Trends;(118) London Express/Pictorial Parade; (119) United Press International; (120, 121) Syndication International/Photo Trends; (124, 125, 128) Michael Cooper; (129) Jim Marshall; (131, 132-133) Eric Hayes; (134-135) Eric Hayes/Collection, Tom Beach; (137, 138-139, 140) Ethan A. Russell/Collection, Geoffrey Cannon; (141) Ethan A. Russell; (143) Michael Cooper; (146) Syndication International/Photo Trends; (147) Ethan A. Russell; (148) Syndication International/Photo Trends; (149) Camera Press/Collection, Tom Beach; (150-151, 153) International/Photo Trends; (154-155) Ethan A. Russell; (156) Joseph Sia; (157, 158-159) Ethan A. Russell; (160-161) Elizabeth Sunflower; (162-163) Ethan A. Russell; (165, 166, 167, 168, 169) Norman Seeff; (170-171) Cecil Beaton/Camera Press; (175, 176, 177, 178-179) Dominique Tarlé; (180-181) Michael Cooper; (182-183) Terry O'Neill; (184-185, 186, 187) Annie Leibovitz; (188, 189) Ethan A. Russell; (190) Peter Beard; (191) Ethan A. Russell; (193, 194, 195) Peter Beard; (196-197) Ethan A. Russell; (198) Annie Leibovitz; (201) Hiro, Courtesy the Rolling Stones; (202-203) Peter Beard; (204) Annie Leibovitz; (205) Peter Beard; (206-207) Hiro; (208, 209, 210, 211, 212-213) Christopher Sykes; (214-215, 216-217, 218, 219) Annie Leibovitz; (220-221) Annie Leibovitz, reprinted by permission of Pantheon Books, a division of Random House, Inc.; (222) Christopher Sykes; (224-225, 226-227, 228-229) Jean C. Pigozzi; (230, 231, 232-233) Annie Leibovitz; (235) D. Shigley/Photo Reserve; (236-237) Baron Wolman; (238-239) Gary Gershoff/Retna; (240-241) Ken Reagan/Camera 5; (242) Jean C. Pigozzi; (243) Annie Leibovitz; (244, 245) Bonnie Schiffman; (246) David McGough/DMI; (247) Jean C. Pigozzi; (248-249) Lynn Goldsmith/LGI; (250) Jean C. Pigozzi; (251) Sheila Metzner; (252-253) Annie Leibovitz; (256) Christopher Sykes.

Michael Cooper and his young son Adam lived with Keith Richards for two years in the late Sixties, during which time he documented the Rolling Stones on and off stage. He died in London in 1973 at the age of 29.

Annie Leibovitz, Rolling Stone's chief photographer, has photographed the Rolling Stones since she joined the magazine's staff in 1970. She is a frequent contributor to Vanity Fair as well as other publications. Her first collection of photographs, Annie Leibovitz Photographs, will be published in 1983.

Gered Mankowitz was commissioned by Andrew Loog Oldham to photograph the Rolling Stones in 1965 and he photographed them frequently until their breakup with Oldham in 1967. Mankowitz currently photographs album covers and works as an advertising and editorial photographer. Hit Parade, a collection of his photographs of contemporary pop stars, will be published in 1983.

Ethan Russell first photographed the Rolling Stones for Rolling Stone magazine in 1968 and continued to photograph them through 1972, touring with them in 1969 and 1972, and photographing the covers of the "Honky Tonk Women" single and Through the Past Darkly. He presently works as a writer and director on music-related film projects.

Mick Jagger with photographer Annie Leibovitz.

This book is set in Kennerly by Mackenzie-Harris of San Francisco, with display in Kennerly by Patrick Pagano of New York.

PICTURE RESEARCH BY ILENE CHERNA.